Born and brought up in South Wales, Joyce moved to Oxfordshire in her early twenties. She later completed a teaching degree and taught children with severe learning disabilities for 22 years.

Always physically active and adventurous, Joyce spent a lot of time walking, in her childhood with her brother on the beaches of South Wales. Later in a local walking group or with friends.

Joyce now lives in West Oxfordshire.

GW00536137

I dedicate this book to the memory of my son Shon who supported and encouraged us during our long walk.

Elizabeth Joyce Davies

TWO OLD LADIES AND A HEDGE

AUSTIN MACAULEY PUBLISHERS™

LONDON • CAMBRIDGE • NEW YORK • SHARJAH

A CIP catalogue record for this title is available from the British Library.

ISBN 9781398444324 (Paperback)
ISBN 9781398444331 (ePub e-book)

www.austinmacauley.com

First Published 2022
Austin Macauley Publishers Ltd®
1 Canada Square
Canary Wharf
London
E14 5AA

Thanks to Karen for her enthusiasm and tenacity in completing our goal.

Synopsis

Two Old Ladies and a Hedge is an account of a walk around the South West Coast Path over a number of years. Many people have accomplished this feat since the path became a popular challenge to serious walkers, runners and holiday makers. What makes this account a little different is that the participants were two elderly women who began the walk in their late sixties and early seventies and completed it when the author was nearing eighty and her companion not far behind. It took a long time to complete the walk due to familial problems and a serious illness suffered by the author.

The account of the walk is also unusual due to the sleeping arrangements practiced. For most of the time comfortable bed and breakfast accommodation was dispensed with and sleeping out in bivvy bags, with a tarpaulin and umbrellas, was the norm. Consequently, luggage was heavy for ageing bodies to carry and ingenuity was developed in order to keep hypothermia at bay during typical British summer and early autumn nights.

As well as the sense of freedom and adventure the challenge gave the participants, it was felt that older people in particular need an objective to look forward to and plan for, or senility can creep in and life can become mundane with doctors' appointments the highlight of the week and current medication the main discussion topic. Of course, everybody needs to choose their own objective and the book is not a call for all, or indeed any, pensioners to follow its lead.

The journey around the path started in earnest in 2012 and finished in September 2020, although, a few sections had been completed before 2012 during holiday breaks in the area. The direction of the route taken was not the conventional one as outlined in most guide books from Minehead to Poole, but generally completed in sections from Poole to Minehead. We often walked in the opposite direction because it was more convenient for public transport in accessing the path.

Finally, one of the rewards of this challenge was the interesting people encountered on the way. These included fellow walkers of various nationalities and ages, authors, a well-known television star, a homeless man, and an interesting mindful sort of hippy as well as friendly locals and welcoming guesthouse owners. It was well worth doing and gave us a unique experience of living close to nature, dealing with the challenges of the elements and rewarding us with a great sense of accomplishment.

Introduction

As a child growing up in the 1940s and '50s before car ownership was the norm, everybody walked more, so you either walked everywhere or you stayed at home. Thus, walking became second nature and you learnt to enjoy it. Also, there is the sense of adventure and challenge which you are either born with or develop as you mature. It was what my friend Karen and I had in common when we decided to walk the South West Coast Path in 2011. Being seventy, Karen a little younger, both quite fit for our ages and both having a love for the outdoors, we decided to set ourselves the challenge of walking a total distance of about six hundred and thirty miles.

Karen and I had met at a local walking group of people over fifty. In fact, most of our fellow walkers were over sixty, some approaching eighty. We both loved walking and the outdoors, both had the restless bug and wanted a challenge but a challenge with a difference. We wanted to experience some adventure before we became too old and infirm to physically and mentally achieve this feat, let alone enjoy it.

We decided to tackle the path after participating in walking sections of it during short trips to Weymouth and Swanage. The section from Sandbanks to Lyme Regis had been completed during these trips, at one point camping at a converted Nissen hut near Swanage. It was decided to walk the coastal path in the opposite direction to the usual route at first, as this was more convenient to us travelling from our homes in Oxfordshire. We had a base in Weymouth for the first section of the path, so we used this for the start. We later walked sections from east to west or vice versa, depending on which direction was most accessible to us at the time. We had to work out where we could sleep and eat and how much we would have to carry. Some parts of the path are isolated and accommodation where we wanted it might be difficult to find.

To reduce the pressure of having to reach places we may have pre-booked and where we might have too far to walk at the end of the day, the idea of using bivvy bags and a tarpaulin was born. This would reduce the stress of being a long way from our B and B and having to rush to get there before dark or when we were feeling very tired. We did not know how far we were capable of walking at the start, carrying our large bags, as so much depended on the terrain and the weather. We became more adept at assessing the distances we were capable of as our journey progressed and we became more experienced in walking on different terrains and in all sorts of weather. The idea of sleeping wild also appealed to our sense of freedom and getting as near to nature as we could possibly get.

It took us nearly ten years, due to unforeseen circumstances which included family bereavements and a personal serious illness, to complete our journey. At the time of planning our great adventure, we had no idea of the tragedies and traumas that would delay the completion of our plans. Nobody can foretell the future and each day must be lived to the full.

Trial and Error

We had completed the coastal path between Sandbanks and Beer in Dorset during short visits to Weymouth and camping at Swanage during 2011. We also tried to experiment with sleeping out without a tent at Lyme Regis. This was our first experience of wild camping. The evening turned out to be overcast and then a fine drizzle began to fall. We walked into the gloomy, dripping woods of the Undercliff carrying our heavy rucksacks. The Undercliff had been formed years ago when a massive landmass had slipped down the cliffs to form an area of almost tropical forest with of dense canopy, twisted trees, creepers and gnarled roots. This vegetation made the path through it difficult to negotiate carrying large rucksacks. We later got more used to carrying such a weight on our backs but the first time was quite a shock to the system. We ventured into the wood looking for a suitable place to lay the tarpaulin in order to position our sleeping bags. We could find no such place as the ground was uneven and filled with roots and undergrowth and the terrain slipped away in a steep slope providing no suitable flat areas. The forecast was for thundery rain, so reluctantly we returned to the field above and agreed to abort our first attempt at wild camping and catch the bus back to Weymouth where we were based.

We had learned our first lessons about sleeping out without a tent. Our rucksacks were so heavy, about 9 or 10 kilograms, that we had to help each other to lift them onto our backs, so we would have to be careful what we packed. A suitable place to lay out our sleeping mats was also crucial. The space we needed was to be on as flat a surface as possible, the grass not too long, no visible thistles or stones and a suitable area around us to arrange our bags, boots and other possessions. Karen turned out to be a master space saver, as I found out later on, she used her rucksack as a pillow and slept in her boots in case we had to make a rapid retreat in the night! The weather obviously played such an important part. Rain was our enemy, warm balmy nights were our friends. During our future escapades we experienced both, the former with a vengeance! We were to gain more experience during our next attempt at trying to cosy up to the elements.

In early September 2012, we tried again. An isolated beach was found on the map. I had visited it in the past and knew it was quite secluded and ideal for our trial. As the weather had been quite warm for the time of year, we naively took one blanket each in order to reduce the weight we would have to carry. Karen had sewn hers into a makeshift sleeping bag. In order to keep dry, I had a large, what I thought to be, waterproof bag, which I had purchased from a charity shop, Karen had a bivvy bag and what was to be her salvation, a double skinned foil survival bag. This she had obtained from her daughter who had used it for her Duke of Edinburgh award years previously. As we planned our first attempt to sleep out without a tent, little did we know what was in store for us!

We caught the bus from Weymouth arriving in Beer around midday. The weather was warm and sunny. We then walked to Boscombe and had a baked potato lunch at the beach cafe. I had a swim and we sat in the sun for a while. We fancied a cup of tea so made our way to a cafe in the idyllic village of Branscombe. Having filled up with chocolate cake and tea we returned to our route making our way to the beach at Weston Mouth. The pebble beach was deserted and the sun beginning to go down. Later that evening feeling peckish we ate some soggy tomato sandwiches which Karen had packed in her rucksack. They tasted so good! A family came to swim but did not stay long as it was beginning to get dark. The temperature dropped and we were beginning to feel chilly. There was dried seaweed and driftwood lying about so I lit some with the lighter I had brought. Karen was a bit alarmed, as she thought it would attract attention to us if anyone was about, so we extinguished it. We laid out sleeping mats and made our beds. snuggling down side by side alongside an upturned boat. It was 8 pm. I had my mobile phone so tuned in to "Any Questions". The temperature began to fall rapidly. Karen struggled into her foil bag. I laughed out loud, she looked like a large chicken ready for roasting. However, she had the last laugh as the bag kept her reasonably warm and I nearly succumbed to hypothermia. The sea was calm and we could see the lights of fishing boats.

Later, probably after midnight, mist came in from the sea wetting my outer bag. During the early morning the temperature dropped to nine degrees. My outer bag, which was not a custom-made bivvy bag proved not to be waterproof and my blanket was damp. I clutched the mosquito head net more tightly around my face to try and secure some extra warmth from it, I felt a weird desire to cut some branches from the wispy bush above me and put them on top of my bedding to add extra warmth. Instead, I crawled out of my bed and sat huddled in my pakamac, draped in the damp blanket until dawn broke. Karen seemed to sleep a bit but I was so cold I had no sleep to speak of, maybe a few minutes dozing. Well, you have to learn by experience, don't you!

Knicker Wading and Umbrellas

The next time we were able to start the path in earnest was in June 2012. Based at Weymouth we used our bus passes to travel via Exeter to Plymouth. We were going to walk in an easterly direction. We crossed The Sound from The Citadel crossing point to Batten Point and made our way along the path. It was drizzling and the rain began to increase in intensity until it was lashing down. We were planning to camp out but this became less appealing with the prospect of sleeping out with no tent in such horrible weather. We had nowhere booked or even emergency addresses we could ring. Plodding on, carrying our ready meals, which we had bought in a corner shop, in a nylon shopping bag tied onto Karen's rucksack, we discussed our dilemma.

The rain eased somewhat and we sat on a grassy bank using our sit mats to eat our evening meal.

'We can use our umbrellas,' said Karen optimistically. We walked on and out of the blue there appeared, what was almost a mirage, a homely looking guest house overlooking a cove. Knocking on the door we were relieved to discover there were vacancies. We were shown to a twin-bedded room overlooking the sea. In fact, we were so close we could hear it crashing on the beach below. We had a shower with the shower head reluctantly dribbling water but we were grateful as we hadn't expected such luxury that night. There was also a conservatory where we could dry our sopping rain jackets.

After a good night's sleep, we left the guest house wearing our dried-out rain jackets and boots and walked towards the Wenbury ferry crossing where we crossed the River Yealm. We did well, walking ten miles until we reached the River Erme. The guide book had informed us that we could wade across the river where it entered the sea. Tentatively, boots draped around our necks, we set forth using our walking poles to steady ourselves against the current and negotiate the pebbles on the river bed. The water rose to above our knees and was in danger of soaking our rolled-up trousers.

'We'll have to take them off,' shouted Karen above the rush of the water.

We stumbled back to the shore, took our trousers off, draped them around our necks with the boots and set off again into the rushing water in our knickers.

More by luck than judgement, the tide was on the ebb so the water did not rise above our thighs and we managed to make the east bank with sighs of relief. A man was making the same crossing lower down the estuary. I wonder what he thought of the sight of two old ladies crossing the river, carrying huge rucksacks, in their knickers! The crossing and the long walk prior to it, had taken its toll, so we sat for about four hours in the sun on the river bank resting, snacking on biscuits and drinking water from our bottles. Oh, for a cup of tea!

As the dusk started to fall, so did a light drizzle.

'It's sea mist,' Karen declared hopefully.

Luckily, the drizzle or sea mist subsided and I wandered up the river looking for a suitable place to bed down whilst Karen looked after the bags. There were some old industrial buildings weathered to a lovely rich pale brown colour but nowhere suitable to sleep. We eventually found a spot near to where we had been sitting and laid out our ground sheets. The camp was backed by a thick hedge with a low canopy of branches above. It was quite secluded which gave us a feeling of security. We got into our sleeping bags early as we were tired after our efforts. We read our books for a while until it got dark. This was our first night out using bivvy bags except for our disastrous attempt at Weston Mouth the year before. During the night we were kept awake by the waves banging and crashing up the estuary but eventually fell asleep. There was a little drizzle in the night but we were covered up by a tarpaulin pegged over both of us and umbrellas placed strategically over our heads.

Dawn broke with the incessant roar of the waves crashing up the estuary. When I woke up, I thought the tendrils from the hedge hanging over me were my bedroom curtains at home. The damp, earthy smell of the grass and weeds in which we were lying was also a new sensory experience. It was a strange new feeling of being at one with nature. We were a bit cold when we woke in the early morning and resolved to invest in better quality sleeping bags as our current ones were not warm enough for the purpose.

After eating our breakfast of biscuits and water, we set off for Bigbury-on-Sea with the hope of finding some more substantial food and a nice cup of tea. Although the distance was only about five miles, the terrain was difficult with massive undulations. We were very thirsty and as we walked through Challaborough, we noticed a holiday park where we were able to buy a bottle of drink each. We eventually reached Bigbury and chatted to some surfing instructors who were impressed by us sleeping out in bivvy bags. Although they were too polite to mention it, it was probably doing it at our age which impressed them!

Stomachs rumbling, we found a beach cafe and devoured Greek salad and chips and the much-awaited cup of tea. On our whole walk of the coastal path, we had to find food where we could. This could prove difficult at times as some sections of the path are wild and desolate with no habitations except, perhaps, remote farm buildings. If we were lucky enough to come across a coastal pub, it was mostly shut until lunchtime, or the village was a few miles off our route which meant diverting and having to return to the path. A camping stove, pans, cutlery etc. were too heavy for us to carry with all our other essential gear, so we relied on finding cafes and pubs where we could. If we were too far out in the wilds and there were none, we resorted to our emergency rations of meal bars, biscuits, any fruit we had managed to save and blackberries we could forage. One of our breakfast staples was packets of porridge mixed with cold water. A cup of tea was usually the first thing we wanted when we woke from our slumbers and we would hurry along the path in the hope that a cafe would be open in the next village.

Leaving Bigbury-on-Sea at about five o'clock, we set off inland for Averton Gifford, a small village where there would be a bus connection to Exeter from where we could make our way to Weymouth using our bus passes. We passed a picturesque gypsy caravan with a "To Let" notice on the fence.

'I would love to stay in that. Do you think it would be available for just one night?' I was as enthused as Karen.

'Let's knock on the door and ask.'

The door was that of a large cottage on the other side of the narrow lane we were on. I knocked at the door and after a long wait, a man appeared. The man said that the owner was not there and we could not rent it. Curiously, we later looked up the advertised phone number and rang up. A man answered and said the caravan was not available.

'It's the same man. I recognise his voice,' Karen observed.

We were disappointed as it was in a beautiful location and would have been a quirky overnight stop. Perhaps, the owner was a bit suspicious of us as we probably looked a sight!

Our old enemy, the rain, began to fall, first with a fine drizzle, then increasing to a steady fall. A woman with dogs came through a field gate as we were recceing for suitable sleeping quarters having almost decided on a place under a large oak tree which seemed to offer some shelter.

'Are you lost?' she enquired, looking dubiously at our huge dripping bags and bedraggled figures.

'Are there any B and Bs in the village?' I asked for something to say.

We had decided to sleep out as the rain was easing a little, but didn't want to shock her too much. She said that she wasn't sure. She hurriedly walked on with the dogs straining on their leashes.

The rain had stopped for the moment and we were a bit lost, so set off up a narrow lane in the hope of finding a suitable sleeping spot away from the village. The lane was aptly named Drunkards' Lane as we felt a little drunk with fatigue. Litter strewed the hedges and a few larger objects such as empty paint cans and old tyres had been discarded in the nettles bordering the lane. It may have been a favourite spot for drunkards, fly tippers, or both, but was not an appealing sleeping location for us. There was no suitable place up the lane, which was incongruous with the surrounding attractive area, so we walked on up and found ourselves in another wider lane which, to the right, went back into the village. We turned left to distance ourselves from possible dog walkers from the village. Getting rather desperate, as the overcast sky forecast darkness falling early, we eventually found a grassy layby on the side of the road.

The map showed no immediate habitation for a few miles up the lane, so we decided we were reasonably hidden as time was getting on. There were a few loose branches strewn about, so we dragged them to block the entrance to the layby. Unfortunately, the rain began to fall in light showers, we seemed to be fated with bad weather, so we placed the ground sheets as near the hedge on the side as possible where the overhanging branches protected us. There was a sort of corrugated tin wall in the hedge which gave us a bit of protection from the wind. Karen suggested hanging the tarpaulin down from it, but there were no suitable points to secure it, so it was decided to wedge the umbrellas in the hedge so they offered a little more protection from the rain. Placing the tarpaulin over our sleeping bags, we crept in. Snug as bugs in rugs, unless a car decided to crash through our defences and mow us down!

Needless to say, I slept fitfully in case I heard a car approaching and slowing down for a turn. There was another anxiety as I listened to the rain pattering on my umbrella. Would the rhythm increase so much that we would be flooded out of our bags? Luckily, this did not happen and the rain lightened to intermittent showers and eventually stopped. We slept, in our unusual bedroom with hedge walls and a partial canopy of branches overlooked by a dark moody sky for our ceiling. Occasionally, if the clouds formed a space, we might see the glimmer of a solitary star.

The morning dawned clear and calm. I lay for a while smelling the dank odour of grass and damp branches. Dew had formed on the tarpaulin and the umbrella dripped drops onto my face if I turned and disturbed it. This morning sensation, which we were becoming familiar with, was a bit different from waking in a soft, warm bed. It was not always unpleasant, especially if sleep had been deep and satisfying.

Karen was stirring and we both heard the wonderful chirruping of a young blackbird perched on a gatepost, so near, I could have touched it. Its mother was calling to it with wonderful trilling notes. It didn't even move when I got out of my bed.

There may have been a certain amount of unconventionality and discomfort about the way in which we were living at the moment, but we were living close to nature and experiencing sights, sounds and smells that stimulated our sensory awareness in such a way that one would not have waking-up in a conventional bed. We felt that we had never been so close to the natural world before, sleeping on the earth, feeling the wetness of dew as the damp grass flicked our faces and hearing the little bird's beautiful sounds filling our ears. We also felt a sense of achievement, making a primitive shelter and actually being able to sleep in it. I expect most septuagenarians would be horrified but then we were not like most septuagenarians!

We had risen early, just after five. We had our first breakfast of the usual biscuits and water hoping that another was to follow when we reached a cafe or village shop which was open, as it was very early yet. Performing our ablutions was quite a task; a token wash using wet wipes, cleaning teeth using a beaker partially filled with our precious water and the awkward performance of putting contact lenses in without dropping them. We both used the soft ones which required cleaning and inserting into the eyes. Napkins were laid on the floor whilst we fiddled with the lenses trying to be as hygienic as we could in the circumstances. I was glad when much later on in our travels I had my cataracts removed and my short sight adjusted so that I could dispense with the lenses.

To perform natural bodily functions, we used, where and when possible, public toilets. As we were often miles away from these amenities, we tended to use off-path, hidden locations, burying, or covering the evidence with leaves, stones or loose earth, whatever was available. We left the sites natural with no evidence of our visits such as discarded tissues. We placed this in doggy bags ready to be disposed of when we found a bin. On our first trial sleepout at Branscombe, I had tried to dig a 'wee' hole with a plastic trowel. This had been unsuccessful as the ground had proved to be too hard. When we later described our adventures, people would often ask how we managed with no running water, bathrooms and other, taken for granted "essentials".

'I couldn't do that!' they would declare with horror.

'Well,' I would reply, 'nobody's asking you to.'

Admittedly, it does sound a little unusual for two old ladies to be setting up camp in a damp layby, after blocking up the entrance with branches, sleeping under umbrellas, but we considered it to be preferable to being at home in an armchair, crocheting squares or knitting socks or doing endless cleaning. Well, we thought so anyway.

After our damp, showery night, we were eager to have a decent breakfast and set off up the road to Averton Gifford where we caught the local bus to Kingsbridge. Here we found a cafe where we had toasted tea cakes and tea which went down a treat. Later on, we caught a series of buses back to Weymouth via Totnes and Exeter. It took us all day, but at least we were sitting down for most of it.

Suggestions and Storms

It was not until early May the following year that we were able to venture forth on the next section of the path. It was early in the year to be sleeping outside, so it was decided to combine inside and outside accommodation, in the form of bed and breakfasts and bivvy bagging. As we were using the National Express coach service from Swindon to Plymouth, with a little bus hopping to start from home, we would not be arriving in Plymouth until early evening.

Having caught a local bus, we arrived at our pre-booked bed and breakfast. During the whole walk, we rarely pre-booked our accommodation, as it could restrict our progress or overshoot our capabilities of arriving there before it got dark or before our stamina wore out. However, occasionally, we appreciated the luxury of a bed and hot shower. This feeling of appreciation was somewhat tinged with the feeling that we were cheating. We wanted to challenge the pre-conceived idea of what older ladies usually did or were capable of doing. I suppose we didn't really want to grow old gracefully and being young in mind and spirit, still wanted to have adventures and experiences not common to our generation at the age we now happened to be.

The next day proved to be quite mild. We caught the ferry to Edgecumbe and had a good day-1 walking through the Kingsand, Cawsand, around Rame Head, then towards Freathy. Little weathered shacks scattered the steep banks and we searched for a place to sleep. It was a little overpopulated for our need to be secluded, but it was getting late and we were tired.

'I wonder who lives in the huts,' Karen pondered.

Indeed, some of them looked in a poor state of repair and there was nobody about.

'Probably holiday homes,' I observed hopefully as we didn't want to be overlooked sleeping out and there was no likely spot in sight.

Eventually, we found a grassy bank near a lifeboat station. 'We should be alright here,' I observed inspecting the area. We were too tired to care so laid out our beds and wriggled in. Wriggled, was the operative word as it was a major operation to get into our sleeping bags, which included a separate liner, mainly for additional warmth. The first wriggling session was to get into the liner. Next you had to pull the sleeping bag, which was inside the bivvy bag up to your neck so that the hood could be pulled over your head. It was quite a workout after all our staggering up cliff paths carrying our heavy bags, in fact, I sometimes felt more exhausted with this performance than the actual walking! Karen also had additional difficulty, as she kept her boots on, encased in a plastic bag in order to try to keep her bedding clean.

As we settled down to sleep in the dusk, with the sound of the sea starting to lull us into oblivion, we heard the sound of voices approaching and the crunch of gravel right next to us.

A group of men passed by with fishing rods. They were going night fishing. 'We're camping,' I quavered in an embarrassed voice. 'Enjoy,' they shouted. They didn't turn a hair, as if it was perfectly normal to see two old ladies, one wearing hair rollers, with her hair covered in a scarf, both with mosquito nets over their heads, stretched out on the bank. Umbrellas were up over our heads and we were covered with a tarpaulin. We were just inches off their path. 'Cor, that gave me a fright. Didn't expect that.' I sniggered. Karen laughed. 'I expect we gave them a fright!' We dozed until we heard them coming back on their way home, flitting past us quietly in the dark. We could see a beaming light out to sea. Looking on the map next day, we found it to be the Eddystone Lighthouse. We watched it lighting up the dark sky. Then we slept.

The morning dawned and the sky lightened with the promise of a fine day. The smell of the sea below our bank, wafted towards us and made us wish for bacon and eggs. Instead, we ate our breakfast of syrup flavoured porridge oats with water, eaten from the packet. Filling up with broken bits of energy bars we had left. We performed our basic ablutions, packed our bags and set off.

The main path led through a large area of requisitioned Army land. This area proved to be a little confusing as offshoot paths diverted here and there. There was no signing that we could see. Finding the right path, we continued on to Seaton, a seaside village favoured by surfers. There was a delightful surfers' cafe waiting for us, where we talked to a party of young men who were fuelling up to join a canoe race to Looe. The bacon and egg baps were delicious. They were washed down with a pot of tea for two, while we sat in the sun and watched the canoeists carrying their boats to the sea and setting off. We could have sat there in the sun for longer but had to get on as we had a few miles to go to reach Looe where we had planned to spend the night.

There was a picnic area with slatted bench type table near the beach just before Looe. Dusk was falling and sea mist rolled in. We sat at the bench and ate our supper consisting of a cold ready meal that had been purchased at a shop on the way. As we were contemplating likely places for our beds to be laid out, a man and dog appeared from apparently nowhere, so we decided the location was too near the adjacent caravan site. Karen got out her phone.

'Let's see if one of the B and Bs has vacancies.'

Prior to starting out on our trips, we always compiled a list and phone numbers of B and Bs in various places on our route, in case of emergencies such as bad weather or too populated locations. These were usually a last resort as we preferred our "wild" locations and unconventional methods of bedding down. Each location was different in its surroundings and provision of shelter, be it a hedge, wall or canopy of trees. This added to our feelings of security and accomplishment in finding a 'good' place. However, this was one of the times when we decided that it was better to sleep "in" rather than "out".

The next morning dawned bright and sunny. We set off in good spirits after an undisturbed sleep with no unexpected interruptions. We walked through Portlooe and Talland stopping to give our backs a rest and admire the beautiful rugged coastline.

'I feel like fish and chips.' Karen licked her lips in anticipation.

'We'll see if we can get some at Polperro, it's not far.'

We had walked for about six miles and were beginning to get hungry. It was an effort to climb up and down the stoney or grassy footpath with what felt like another person on our backs. Although as time went on, we did get more used to carrying the heavy rucksacks, but were always relieved to unstrap them and collapse onto the ground beside them. We suddenly became light and free. Karen was a bit concerned that she might become permanently bent over and she tried to walk in a more upright position using her walking poles when carrying the bag. I just pulled the support strap around my waist tighter so that the weight seemed to be pushed up instead of dragging down.

Arriving at the pretty village of Polperro, we sat on a seat overlooking the harbour and ate fish cakes and chips with relish. Fancying a cup of tea, we moved onto a seat outside the museum carrying our steaming mugs.

'Where are you off to?' The voice came from one of two youngish men who were sat on an adjacent seat. We explained what we were doing and they were astounded that we were doing it at our advanced ages.

'You ought to write a book,' one of them declared enthusiastically. We laughed and titles were discussed. 'Two Old Ladies and a Hedge! That's it.'

So, the idea was conceived. They also advised us to invest in down sleeping bags after their experience of using them during sleepovers. I don't think they were the camping sorts.

Time was getting on, so saying goodbye to our two friends, we humped our bags onto a convenient wall so that we could manoeuvre ourselves into the array of staps. Setting off up the road we found the path again. It was beginning to become overcast and the wind was getting up.

'Don't like the look of this. It's coming in from the sea.' I was not looking forward to a night out in bad weather. It was getting gloomy and we had to find somewhere suitable to sleep. As usual we were quite hungry and Karen thought that we should try and eat before settling for the night. She found it difficult to sleep on an empty stomach. There was a village called Lansallos just off the path and it had a pub. The rain had begun to fall in little threatening bursts. As we went to the bar to order we had a shock.

'We have finished serving,' said the landlord. 'We've got crisps.

'We're starving, couldn't you rustle up something?'

He took pity on us.

'Alright, I can do you a ploughman's.'

We thanked him profusely and found a cosy table. We were tired as we had walked at least nine miles. The pub was warm and relaxing, but we had to leave to find our outdoor bedroom.

Outside, the rain was beginning to get quite heavy. We walked up a steep bank and looked desperately around. There was a wire fence enclosing a field of sheep. It was getting more threatening as the rain fell and the wind was rising. Tying the tarpaulin to the top of the wire fence, we looked for anchoring points on the ground. The site was on a slope facing out to sea. There were some low gorse bushes at the foot of the tarpaulin and I used them to hold tie the guy ropes to. We had just got under the shelter when the rain lashed in from the sea. The wind blew in huge gusts and the sea roared below. We struggled to lay out our bedding in the confined space under the tarpaulin and got into our bags with extreme difficulty, tying ourselves up in knots in the process. Amazingly, we kept reasonably dry, dragging bits of our equipment, which were exposed, under cover during the night. I kept having to shuffle myself up as I was slipping down the slope towards exposure to the elements. It didn't help that I had a silk liner which acted as a sort of slide. Karen kept complaining that she was lying on a lump and rolled about trying to get comfortable. Meanwhile, the rain lashed down, the tarpaulin flapped alarmingly and we heard the distant grumble of thunder. It was so exciting!

Emerging from a fitful sleep we lay talking for while discussing our next moves. The air smelt damp and grassy with a slight odour of animal dung. Sheep bleated in the field behind the fence.

'We had better move before the farmer comes to feed them, or whatever they do,' I suggested.

We had a quick freshen up using wet wipes and decided to postpone teeth cleaning until after our biscuit breakfast. We didn't want the farmer to catch us dismantling our tarp from his fence.

Later, we sat on the bank at the edge of the path and ate our biscuits before continuing on towards Polruan about four miles away. Here we had a second breakfast at a cafe before catching the ferry to Fowey. The town was very attractive with narrow streets and interesting buildings and shops. The weather had improved and the sun was shining. The route went through the town and onto a promenade towards the site of the castle. A man caught us up.

'I'm intrigued, you look as if you are going a long way,' he exclaimed.

He told us that he walked a bit and was staying at a house on our way.

'Put the coffee on,' Karen suggested cheekily.

Waving to us, he walked on. We continued at a slower pace. As we approached a small cove, we heard a voice calling to us.

'Come and have a coffee.'

We looked around and saw the man we had met beckoning to us from a lovely garden. He indicated a table and chairs and invited us to sit down on an attractive patio in front of an old building. Out came his wife to meet us and we were served with our preferred tea and biscuits. He informed us that the building was the "Boat House" used to model the one in Daphne Du Maurier's famous novel *Rebecca*. The big house "Menabilly" was the model for Du Maurier's "Manderley" where *Rebecca* was set. It was glimpsed through the trees. The man and his wife were either friends or family of the present owners of the big house. I had read *Rebecca* years ago and was thrilled that we were actually sitting outside the "Boat House". I wonder what Mrs Danvers, the fictional, controlling housekeeper at "Manderley", would have thought of us sitting in the "Boat House" garden having tea.

As evening approached, we slept out on the side of the path near the village of Polkerris with no storms to interrupt our sleep. Next morning, we managed to get a huge bacon and egg breakfast for a ridiculously small price in a sort of transport cafe near a large caravan site. Later, I had a swim in the sea at Par Sands to freshen up and nearly got bowled over by the large waves. Karen had more sense and just paddled to wash her feet. We made our way to the delightful village of Charlestown from where we caught the local bus to Plymouth. Here we caught up with civilisation and slept in a bed and breakfast before returning to our homes using the National Express coach and local buses.

Hay Fever and Good Samaritans

In June 2014, we managed to go to the path again. After a day travelling, we reached St Austell in the early evening and set off for Charlestown not far down the road. Arriving in Charlestown we decided to look for a sleeping place beyond the village. There was another village and holiday camp not far along the path and the area was too built up for the privacy we needed. A few miles on the landscape became more sparsely populated and a wild heather covered headland beckoned. The heather was not in bloom at this time of the year but provided us with a springy mattress to sleep on. In fact, it was bliss after our long day to sink down in the gathering dusk and see the lights out to sea, smell the salt air and just catch the twinkle of stars as we fell into a restful slumber.

The next day dawned bright and sunny. We walked the path through magnificent rugged scenery and quaint villages until we reached Mevagissey. We visited the ancient chapel at Chapel Point and found a place to sleep on a headland a few miles along the path. In the morning we had a small breakfast but felt hungry and wondered where we should find somewhere to eat as the area was so remote. There were a few caravan sites on our route but it was so early and there were no other places to eat.

As we approached the village of Portloe, Karen saw a notice pinned to a tree trunk. It informed us that there were refreshments in the form of sandwiched, rolls and hot drinks for sale in Portloe a mile or so along the path. The notice informed us that food was available at a cottage with a stable door up the main street. It was still too early for pubs to be open and we could see no cafes or grocery stores, so intrigued, we went up the street and found the stable door. I knocked and a lady appeared.

'It's a bit early, but do you do food?' I asked hopefully. She informed us that we were a little early, but if we gave her about 30 minutes, she would make us something. Gratefully, not believing our luck, we ordered our usual bacon rolls with brown sauce in my case and mugs of tea. She said that she could make us a packed lunch, too, if we wanted one as there was no habitation for miles. We ordered filled rolls and the kind lady offered us some complementary cake to add to our lunch and filled our water bottles.

Making good progress, we eventually arrived in the hamlet of Piece where we crossed the estuary to St Mawes and Falmouth. It was good to sit on the ferry and have a rest after all our walking. We also enjoyed the relief of having the weight of the rucksacks off our backs.

'I feel like I'm floating.' Karen straightened her shoulders and fluttered her arms.

'Watch you don't float off the boat. I haven't got the strength to dive in and save you.'

We looked at the water churning below us. Yes, we did enjoy our little respite. Falmouth was busy. Food was available so we had a good meal, something we had to take advantage of when we could. Continuing along the coast via the impressive Pendennis Castle and point, we made for Helford Passage to cross again in the ferry. This was a most beautiful estuary. The weather was warm and the river was clear.

'I'm going to have a swim and do some laundry at the same time,' I declared.

'I'll have a rest and watch.'

Karen was not as keen as I was in wild swimming. Removing my bra, as I didn't want too much washing to carry, I plunged in wearing the rest of my clothes including socks.

The water was delightful, clear and so refreshing. Karen couldn't resist and paddled, washing her socks at the same time. There were bleached skeletons of branches on the little beach which we used to hang the clothes from. They dripped in the hot sun while we rested. We had to get moving, as we had another ferry crossing to make before we made for St Kaverne where we would sleep out ready to catch local buses back to Falmouth next morning. Now the problem was what to do with my washing. It was partially dry so I attached it to my rucksack using clips and safety pins which I had brought for emergencies. What I must have looked like I don't know with trousers, T shirt, socks and knickers dangling down my back. I didn't care much either as we rarely met many hikers in more isolated locations on the path. Karen had only washed her socks so wasn't so loaded. I walked in leggings as I had only brought one pair of trousers due to having to be economical with weight.

Arriving at St Anthony in Meneage, a small hamlet, we saw a notice on the wall by a small jetty. We were to hail the ferry from wherever it was on the river or on the other side. We hailed and a small rowing boat approached.

'I hope we don't capsize it with our bags,' Karen said nervously.

I agreed, as I had my washing still dangling. Stuffing some of it into my rucksack, we clambered on board and set off, hoping we wouldn't sink. We made it to the opposite side which was the little hamlet of Flushing.

'That will be three pounds.'

The boat man tied up the rowing boat and we clumsily disembarked quite relieved that the crossing had been achieved successfully without the boat being upturned by two unsteady women carrying heavy, wobbly loads. Now we had to walk towards St Kaverne about two miles away and find a place to sleep.

Approaching the village, we found that it was rather built up with pleasant houses, large gardens and cultivated footpaths leading around and through the area.

'We'll have to go on a bit.' Karen stopped and looked around.

It was too populated for us to sleep here. We were quite tired as we had walked a long way and been swimming in the sea, not to mention our precarious rowing boat trip. We sat in the churchyard on a seat, ate a meal bar each and discussed our position. We even eyed up the seats in the churchyard as suitable beds, but thought we had better not.

The time of the year meant that the evenings were long before darkness fell. This was fine when we were in an isolated place as we could prepare for bed, struggle into our bedding and read our books while it was still light. However, we couldn't do this if someone, usually a dog walker, came strolling along and came across a pile of sleeping bags, tarpaulins, bin bags containing boots and two mosquito netted heads covered with umbrellas sticking out of the bags. It would have been enough to send some people running in the opposite direction in panic! As our days were long, due to having to rise at the crack of dawn, we were usually ready to lie down and rest in the early evening.

As we walked out of the village, we found that possible places to sleep were too overlooked, too near the road or too obviously private. The surrounding terrain was rather flat with large, neat fields. Eventually, we came across a large newly cut wheat field. We made for the far end of the field by the surrounding hedge and set up our camp there. There was a farm building a few fields away and we hoped they were not looking out of the windows with binoculars. Darkness fell, I found it more and more difficult to breathe, it was the dreaded hay fever made worse by the newly cut crop. I had brought a nose spray which gave me some relief, but struggled until the colder air of the morning meant I managed to get some sleep.

Luckily, we were not discovered by the farmer and hurriedly packed our bags and made a hasty retreat as dawn came. We made our way back to the village where we had about a two hour wait for the local bus to Helston. We sat on a seat in the village square opposite the bus stop. After about an hour a man emerged from a gate from one of the houses bordering the square.

'Good morning, can I help you?' he asked politely.

We explained that we were waiting for the bus and as he appeared to live in the adjacent house asked if he could fill our water bottles. He went into his house and emerged with two bottles of water. We asked if there was a cafe in the village.

'There is a shop which sells made up rolls,' he informed us. 'Would you like a cup of tea or coffee?'

We could have hugged him. He went back into his house and emerged carrying two steaming mugs of tea. We thanked him profusely and settled to drink the tea and wait for the shop to open.

Stuffing the appetising looking rolls and other supplies into our bags, we boarded the bus. We were surprised to see it was a mini-bus and already had a good few locals on board. They chatted to us asking where we were going and where we were from. They were very interested and informed us that they were off to a jumble sale in Helston. One lady produced some garments and held them up.

'What size are you?' she demanded of Karen. Karen told her and the lady said, 'They'll fit you. I was taking them to the jumble but you can have them.'

Karen declined gracefully, explaining that she had too much to carry but thanking her for her generous thought.

The bus rolled into Helston and we said goodbye to the friendly locals. We ate our rolls before boarding the bus to Falmouth. The town was as busy as before and we went to the beach for a swim. We were going to spend the night at the backpacker's hostel before going back home. The hostel proved to be very welcoming and terrific value for money. We had a twin-bedded room with a simple breakfast for about sixteen pounds each.

As we were leaving quite early, the warden said that he would leave bread, cereal etc. for us to help ourselves in the morning. Unfortunately, we were about too early and seeing some provisions on the table helped ourselves. I fancied some luxurious looking muesli.

'Mm, this looks nice stuff.' I spooned out some muesli into a bowl and we made some toast using the wholesome grainy bread. We sat down and ate our breakfast. The warden appeared and put some sliced bread on the side table alongside the cornflakes and left the room. A group of mature people arrived and proceeded to fill their bowls with the muesli, looking suspiciously at us.

'Was that your muesli?' I asked guiltily. It turned out that we had eaten some of their supplies which they had left on the table the night before. We apologised, and they accepted with apparent humour, but underneath, I think they were annoyed that we had helped ourselves to their supplies. We made a hasty, embarrassed retreat from the kitchen. We hadn't eaten much of their supplies, we consoled ourselves, and there was plenty left for them. We left the hostel and made our way to coach stop to travel to Swindon via Bristol. From there we bus hopped back to our homes.

Vagrants and Dogs

Due to unexpected illness in my family and the stress of having to deal with it, we were not able to return to the path until the following June. As usual the weather forecast was not very promising. We seemed to be jinxed with bad weather. Maybe the gods were trying to tell us not to be so silly, at our ages, to be trying to sleep outside in such a primitive fashion. The coach we caught from Oxford did not arrive in Helston until 7.15 in the evening. Torrential rain was pouring down and rivulets of water gushed down the street. The weather was much worse than we had thought it would be.

'What are we going to do? Let's get under cover and think,' Karen suggested as we alighted from the bus with our bags shocking our systems into life after sitting on the coach for hours.

There was a large church porch near the bus stop so we sheltered underneath. A middle-aged gentleman was sheltering with us. He was reasonably dressed and carried a holdall but was obviously a vagrant of sorts. we got into conversation with him and told him what we were doing, walking the coastal path sleeping out when we could, with no prior bookings for B and Bs. There was a bus shelter down the road which I subconsciously earmarked as a possible

43

shelter and pointed it out to Karen, but it became obvious that he had his eye on this too and he hurried off in the direction of the bedroom so we discounted it as a possible retreat for the night.

We decided to phone up the vicar of the church as there was a number displayed in the porch. We were desperate and wanted to see if we could sleep inside the church or at least under the porch. A lady, the vicar's wife, answered and suggested we tried The Angel up the road. Apparently, the church does offer vagrants hot showers and light refreshments but not overnight accommodation, perfectly understandable. We managed to get a B and B at the hotel for the night otherwise we would have been in dire straits with the only "free" accommodation that we could see nearby in the town already claimed. Our friend the vagrant had informed us that there was a popular place to stay overnight nearby. This was a ruin of some sort but offered a shelter from the rain. However, we were a bit concerned who we would be sharing it with.

We caught the local bus to St Kaverne and walked to the coast. The heavy rain of the previous night had stopped and everywhere was shrouded in mist so we were unable to see much on the path and or out to sea. We continued along the coast path past Dean Quarries and noticed a jetty which we discovered was used up until 2008 to transport stone and gravel by sea. The quarry had existed in the 1890s and it was proposed to restart it. It was a good example of how the stone, gravel, clay and mineral industries, with their stark reminders of waste heaps and tin mine shaft buildings, co-exist with the beautiful rugged coastal scenery of the area. They add to the atmosphere of Cornwall and provide evidence of a rich industrial history. This goes hand in hand with today's mostly tourist trade and tells the visitor about the area's past enterprises and possible future developments.

Along the cliffs I noticed a man peering over.

'Look at the seals.' He pointed to the beach well below to where we were standing.

About six seals were being released into the sea. The leader was reluctant and kept turning around and slithering back towards his keepers who waited by large cages. Eventually, one by one, they entered the sea and bobbed away getting smaller and smaller. We waited until the last one had become a small dot way out in the ocean. They had probably come from the seal sanctuary at Greek up the Helford River a few miles away. Not long after we were treated to another wildlife spectacle in the form of a school of dolphins not far out to sea. What wonderful treats the Lizard peninsular had given us in one day.

Continuing along the path, we reached Coverack and stopped for coffee. Light rain started and as we approached the Lizard peninsular it increased to become a steady downpour which continued all day. Karen's waterproof was more effective than mine, which was leaking a bit, so I pulled a large, yellow cycling cape on top of my pakamac which caused problems by ballooning out, especially when climbing over stiles.

'It's a wonder I don't take off.'

I shouted above the wind which had begun to increase. The cape almost parachuted me over as I negotiated a style. Climbing over styles had to be done with great caution. We would throw our poles over first then climb over trying not to be overbalanced by our bags. It was great when the barrier was in the form of a gate. However, sometimes we got wedged in a too narrow opening and had to take the bags off to get through. We would often wonder how a very overweight person would manage.

We sheltered in Black Rock Tower, a wildlife viewing building, which provided some welcome respite from the weather. Here we ate our rolls which we had purchased at Coverack. Even with the rain falling we were able to appreciate the beautiful, wild scenery of the Lizard. The mist was heavy and everything was obscured. As evening approached, the weather improved. The rain stopped and we found a place to bed down. It was quite easy to find a spot this time, as the landscape was deserted possibly due to the rainy day, we had had which did not attract visitors.

We had a good night's sleep and woke about at about five-thirty. The down sleeping bags we had invested in on the advice of the two men we had met at Polperro, proved to live up to their recommendations. We both felt warm and cosy when we awoke. We had been in bed since about nine the previous night, so had had enough sleep. It took us at least an hour to perform our ablutions, have a breakfast snack and pack our bags. We always tidied up the site even rearranging the grass at times. No trace was left as to where we had settled. We were like Cornish piskies who flitted away by dawn!

At Cadgwith, luckily, we found a beach cafe open and sat down to our favoured bacon and egg sandwiches with a pot of tea. The beach was used by surfers, but they had not yet appeared, so we were served immediately. We enjoyed these early morning breaks where we could sit admiring the view and discuss our plans for the day.

Continuing along the cliffs, the day proved to be good, sunny with a cool sea breeze. The route was undulating with spectacular views. Later we stopped at the cafe near Lizard Point and had a filled baked potato which we ate hungrily as we looked at the magnificent view outside. Sleeping arrangements were discussed. Having passed a Youth Hostel, we dissuaded the idea of seeing if there was any room. It looked crowded as there were lots of young people milling around it.

Dormitory sleeping arrangements did not appeal to either of us unless in an emergency. We had had an experience in a dormitory, at one hostel a year or two previously, when a loud snorer kept Karen awake so much that she escaped to the common room in the middle of the night and slept on the settee. Being an early riser, I quietly crept into the room, to read my book for a while until breakfast and was surprised to find Karen sleeping there. At least she was sleeping until I woke her up!

'How could you sleep through that?' she asked incredulously.

I suppose I had been so tired I could have slept through anything. Anyway, the weather was getting better and the rain had stopped, so the idea of the hostel was abandoned.

As evening approached, we started to look for possible sleeping places. This takes time as we do not want to be too near the path in case someone comes along. Sometimes the path runs too near the cliff edge or there is a fence or tight hedge of gorse alongside with no wide border for us to use. We would often find really suitable places as we walked on the way, but it was often too early in the afternoon. This looking for good sites becomes a sort of habit, as we both admitted to scouring the landscape for them even when not on the path. Sometimes we would look for them on a country walk near home, or even from the top deck of a bus which we frequently used. We needed space in which we could position our ground sheets and bivvy bags. This space must be of a suitable surface e.g., grass, heather, sand even shingle where there is no choice. We then positioned the tarpaulin ready to creep under.

A place was found near Kynance Cove well up on the cliffs. We found a field with long unkempt grass.

'If we go into the middle we'll be well hidden from the path.' Karen looked around and had a recce of the field. 'We should be alright here.' She indicated a thistle-free area and we set up our camp.

Settling down in our beds to read for a while before dark, we were ready to drop off. Suddenly we heard the sound of a vehicle approaching. It was coming closer and eventually stopped near to the wire fence surrounding the field. We waited for our eviction orders, but they did not come. At one point I nearly decided to reveal ourselves and see if the farmer, or whoever it was, would take pity on us and let us remain. There were two voices. We could hear them very near us. Lying as flat as we could, they did not seem to have seen us and started banging stakes or gate posts into the ground. Eventually, they stopped and drove away. We felt elated. They hadn't seen us. It felt like we were fugitives who had escaped the enemy, instead of two old ladies sleeping in a field they probably shouldn't have been in.

After our breakfast, we set off towards Kynance Cove. The terrain was quite challenging and we traversed the cove by steep climbing down and up steep rocky steps. We found this very difficult carrying our heavy bags. We decided that we wouldn't have been able to do it without our walking poles. They helped to balance us and aid our progress. It was so important for us at our ages and indeed at any age, to take time to accomplish the task of walking up or down steps or climb over styles. A fall might end up with us having to delay or abandon our trip, in the worse scenario, so we proceeded with caution.

The difficult terrain led to us taking a wrong path and we ended up on a craggy pinnacle with no way forward.

'We've gone the wrong way. This is too "hairy",' said Karen who was leading.

I was stuck on the top of a rock with Karen below. I felt weak and doddery as the bag was over balancing me.

'Take your bag off and pass it to me.' Karen held up her arms ready to receive the heavy appendage.

Sliding it down to her I felt more in control and clambered down from my ridiculously, dodgy position.

'The path should be more obvious,' I grumbled.

'Well, I don't suppose it caters for doddery old girls like us.' Karen laughed.

The false path appeared to be a sort of viewing lookout for fit young hikers, but even they might have found it difficult. Somewhere else on the path we had a similar experience, clambering up a steep, rain wet path, with a loose scree surface, which I thought was too dangerous to be the official path. As we staggered to the top, there was a notice pinned to a tree, "Alternative Path".

The official path proved to be easy walking with wide expanses of short grass scattered with large boulders, ideal sleeping spots but too early to look. At Mullion Cove, we had another filled baked potato, this was one of our staples, as was bacon and eggs. Neither of us ate bacon and eggs much as part of our usual diet, but we found we craved them whilst walking the path. Probably we needed the protein as they filled us up for quite long periods. Similarly, the potatoes filled us up with carbs with a protein filling such as tuna or meaty chilli.

Heading towards Mullion Cove, we found the toilets closed so walked on to the village of Mullion. Here to our relief the toilets were open. We had a nice freshen up then sat in the square to wait for the bus to Helston. Here we were going to sleep before returning to Oxford by coach the next morning. The next objective, when we got to Helston, was where to sleep. At least the weather was dry, not like our previous torrential visit.

Arriving at Helston in the late afternoon, we had to find a sleeping venue. The homeless man we had encountered last time, had told us about a place sometimes used by "outdoor" people to sleep. It appeared to be ruins which provided some sort of shelter. We set off along a lane in the direction he had explained. We walked about half a mile to no avail. We found nothing. Anyway, did we fancy sleeping out in a place possibly frequented by people with possible alcohol or drug problems? The man who we had met on our previous visit had been friendly and appeared to be intelligent. He said that he had been a teacher and maybe had fallen on hard times or had an addiction problem. It would have been good to have found out more about his story.

Evening was rapidly approaching, so we returned to Helston where we knew there was a large country park. Perhaps we could find a place to sleep there. The park ran down the Loe Valley. There was a river running through it and into a large lake. We looked along the river for a likely place. The town adjoined the park, well within walking distance, but further down the valley it was less frequented by dog walkers. We sat on the grass to eat our supper, some filled rolls and a cardboard beaker of tea. We waited a long time until dusk began to fall and the occasional walkers diminished to virtually none. It was getting a bit cold so we decided to bed down in a small copse alongside the path. Laying our bedding down, we climbed in and settled for the night. We heard a scrabbling and a large dog appeared coming towards us to investigate.

'Shoo, go away!' I whispered waving my arms.

We waited for the dog owner to appear and discover us. Luckily, the dog lost interest and scurried back to its owner. 'That was close.' Karen pulled her hood over her head. 'We probably frightened him.' She laughed with her large hair rollers visible under the mosquito head net.

We packed up early in the morning as we didn't want to be discovered by any more dogs or their owners and walked towards the town. A shelter alongside the deserted boating lake provided us with seating where we could freshen up and eat some biscuits and fruit, to tide us over until we could buy something to eat when the shops opened. We sat in the shelter for a while waiting for the shops to open. Luckily, there was a convenient shop selling hot drinks. We bought a welcome cup of tea each just before we boarded the coach back to Oxford. It was a long trip back changing at Plymouth and Bristol. We arrived in Oxford at 7.30 pm but at least we were sitting down for most of it, a rest from bag humping and sleeping under a hedge.

Starry Skies and Cows

In August, the same year we returned to Helston and caught the bus to Mullion where we had finished our last section of the path. We slept on a headland near Polduh Cove under a tall Marconi memorial tower. We were overlooked by what appeared to be a large hotel, but as there were no windows lit up, we presumed it was unoccupied. We later found out that it was training hotel, so there may not have been courses taking place on the night we were there.

It was exposed on the headland but there was nowhere else with suitable cover nearby so we settled down in the lee of the tower. I went to sleep almost instantly but Karen witnessed a clear sky lit by a myriad of stars. She saw shooting stars and when she told me about it in the morning, I complained that she should have woken me up to see such a spectacle. On our nocturnal adventures we often saw the twinkling lights from fishing boats and sometimes flashes from lighthouses. This had been a particularly clear night and the milky way spectacular.

We lunched next day on our way at a lovely cafe set in pine woods overlooking the turquoise sea. It felt like we were on a luxury holiday in some exotic destination so beautiful was the location. I had a swim at Praa Sands, a popular surfing beach. The swell was so great it knocked me off my feet and spun me like being in a washing machine. It was not a great experience but at least I felt clean. Karen wisely just had a paddle. Later we looked for somewhere to sleep. It took ages as the path was narrow with hedges close up to the edge on the landward side and a sheer drop on the seaward side. By the time we found somewhere suitable near Cudden Point, we had walked thirteen and a half miles. Not bad since we were carrying loads of ten kilos on our backs.

Finding a field which was flat with short grass, we set up our camp near the perimeter hedge. There were cows in some of the surrounding fields, but none in our field. We hadn't noticed a large gap in one of the hedges and as we prepared to settle down with our books, Karen gasped. 'Look, there's blinking cows.'

Indeed, there they were, a line of them coming through the gap towards us, looking frisky. Hastily we slung all the bags, beds and books onto the tarp and dragged the lot through the gate at the bottom of the field sighing with relief that we had made it. The cows settled down to graze and splatter in our recent bed space and we packed as best we could and set off to find a new sleeping place.

The dew was heavy that night and as we had slept in a field among quite long grass our gear suffered. This field was all that we could find after our eviction by the cows. In the morning, the tarpaulin was soaked and some water had penetrated into our inner bedding. Stuffing it all into bin bags inside our rucksacks, we set off towards Marazion.

'Let's find a place for breakfast. I need sustenance,' Karen said.

We had eaten our first breakfast of syrup flavoured porridge oats in cold water but this was not enough for long. We found a cafe at Perranuthnoe and ordered our usual fancy of bacon and egg baps washed down with tea.

Energy restored; we resumed our walk to Marazion. Here we spread the tarp and bedding out on the beach to dry, as the day was warm and sunny. We took up a large section of the beach, but it was not very crowded so nobody complained. We had a swim one at a time, the other person guarding our possessions and later sat and ate ice creams as we watched the world go by.

Arriving at the Penzance Backpackers in the late afternoon, we found that we had to share a dormitory with two Asian girls. Looking doubtfully at the top bunks on which we would have to sleep, I didn't relish the thought of clambering up the ladder to get in. We were not keen on sharing due to lack of privacy and the possibility of being confined with a "snorer". One of the girls, who were both saying their prayers, kneeling on the floor, immediately realised my predicament of climbing the steep ladder into the bunk. She kindly offered to swap her bottom bunk for mine. Her friend did the same for Karen. We gratefully accepted their thoughtful offers. They probably thought that at our great ages our needs were greater than theirs. They were from the Middle East, and were studying civil engineering at a northern university. Good for them I thought. The next morning, we returned to Oxford, to our own beds, without the unexpected visitation of cows as our sleepover guests.

Cream Teas and Cosy Camp

The next time we came to Penzance, we thought we would walk as far as we could in the little time before dark and sleep out. Walking through Mousehole, we found a place at the top of a beach, above the tide line, we hoped. A man and a boy came along the beach on an evening walk. The boy approached us and stood in front of us staring and making little noises. He appeared to be a child with special needs and found us fascinating. His father smiled and we had a few friendly words and they walked off. They were probably staying in the hotel nearby and the man was giving his son a last walk before bed. Nobody else came and darkness fell.

In the morning we spread our sea mist wetted tarp and bedding out on the flat rocky beach to dry. When we left after we had breakfasted, I forgot to pick up my pillow and from then on had to improvise with rolled up clothes. Passing the beautiful Lamorna Cove with its steep descent and ascent the walk was a feast of rugged cliffs with spectacular view points. This was a very tough section and we found the huge undulations very difficult with our heavy back packs. Such was the terrain, we sometimes only managed eight or nine miles a day.

As twilight was beginning to fall and the wind was getting up, we started to look for a flattish place. There were none and we ended up on top of a small rocky headland with not much space. With the wind blowing mercilessly, we scrunched down in an uncomfortable position behind a large rock on top of a pinnacle. There was nowhere else as the path was narrow and the seaward drop steep. The rock gave us a little shelter but we couldn't put the umbrellas up in case they blew away. Even if we pegged them down, they would have blown inside out. During the night I kept slipping down the slope we were on and in the end had to place my rucksack by my feet to stop myself rolling. There was a gorse bush near my feet and the bag wedged into this and stopped me rolling. We spent a restless night dozing, with the wind gusting around us and the waves crashing below us.

All day we continued along the cliff, arriving at Porth Curno and the open air Minack Theatre. The place was busy with tourists but we wanted to see the theatre so made our way up the precarious rock steps in order to view it from outside. It was almost like climbing a cliff path, the steps were so steep. Eventually, we looked over the wall and saw the theatre below. It would have been lovely to watch a performance, but there were none until later and I think they had to be pre-booked. So, we said goodbye to Porth Curno and set off in the direction of Porthgwarra where we hoped to find somewhere to eat. Our luck was in, as just off the path we came across a lovely old rectory garden which served cream teas. The owner was interested in our travels and took a photo of us together.

As was our frequent evening fate, the weather took a turn for the worse as we left the rectory and continued along the path. The area was isolated which suited our requirements but the weather did not. Clouds grew grey and threatening and the sea breeze which had been gentle, turned into gusts. There was a drystone wall running along the path, with rough neglected looking fields on the other side.

'We could see what it's like over the wall,' said Karen. 'At least we will be out of the wind there.'

Climbing the wall, I looked over.

'It's a bit rough but we could find a better place if we keep looking over and the wall will protect us from the wind.'

We walked down the side of the wall, clambering up where it was possible in order to view the layout.

Eventually, a place was found. The grass was long and there were a few thistles, but we could bash it down a bit to make a space. Tying the tarp guy ropes to bunches of grass and strong heather fronds growing on top of the wall, we secured the bottom with tent pegs driven into the patches of earth we could find among the grass. Because we have brought a smaller tarp this time, expecting better weather, the length of our tent did not allow much room for our feet, so these remained, encased in our bivvy bags, sticking out beyond the tarp. Still, we were satisfied with our structure.

As soon as we got our beds made up in the space, which was quite roomy width wise, the rain began to patter down. Umbrellas were paced at each end and we felt quite cosy. We even had a bedside table, in the form of a large boulder between us. I made use of it to place my head torch, book and water bottle on it. It was like home from primitive home. The rain continued for most of the night. We tried to curl our legs up to avoid them getting too wet, but they kept reasonably dry in the bivvy bags.

Next morning, we made our way towards Land's End. We passed a small cove and to our surprise there was a little cafe which appeared to be open. It was early, about eight thirty, and as we were in such an isolated location wondered who would use it. Nevertheless, we never missed an opportunity for a cuppa. As we approached, we saw that there was a young man sitting at one of the wooden benches drinking a cup of tea. He looked as bedraggled as us.

'Bad weather last night. We were out in it,' I said in a friendly way.

He laughed. 'So was I.'

We became animated bombarding him with questions. It appeared that he was a fellow bivvy bagger. A rare species. His name was Shaun. He was a lorry driver from Bristol who had decided to take time off to walk the South West Coastal Path. He was walking in the opposite direction to us, from Minehead to Sandbanks. He had got soaked sleeping out the night before, whilst we were in our superior camp behind the wall. The lady running the cafe had taken pity on him and was drying out his clothes in her dryer. We drank our tea together sharing our experiences. When we got up to leave, he gave each of us a hug. It's not often two old ladies can share similar experiences with a young man. We all felt that we belonged to the same club. Waving goodbye to Shaun, we set off towards Land's End.

We hoped to get a decent meal as it seemed ages since we had eaten one. We found the place unattractive and commercialised. Trippers milled around queuing for hot dogs and other junk food. We eventually landed up with a mediocre jacket potato and finished with an ice cream lolly each. We had to dry our bedding and the weather had taken a turn for the better and was warm and sunny. Finding a large area of grass away from the built-up area, we laid out our tarp, ground sheets, sleeping bags and liners on the grass. My silk liner kept blowing away and ended up hooked up on gorse bushes. I carefully disentangled it and weighed it down on the grass with my bag. Passers-by looked at us curiously, no doubt thinking we were illegal immigrants or other such suspicious characters. However, nobody challenged us and we later packed up our dry gear and sat on the grass as far away from the trippers as possible.

Prior to leaving Oxford, we had found out that there was a seasonal bus service between Penzance and Land's End, which was very fortunate for us. We sat about until it was due, then caught it back to Penzance where we had pre-booked a night at the Backpackers before returning to Oxford the next day.

Posh Fish and Chips
and Photo Shoots

We returned to Land's End to continue our walk-in early September the same year. After spending the night at Penzance Backpackers, we caught the open top bus to Land's End. Here we alighted, rather windswept from our open position on the top deck. Hoisting the bags onto our backs after lifting them onto a wall to aid the manoeuvre, we set off for Sennen Cove in search of lunch. As we approached the cove, we looked out for somewhere to eat. It was a surfers' beach and many of them were riding the waves skilfully taking off and landing like large black birds. Further along Whitesand Bay, we spotted a restaurant with a canopied roof right on the beach. It looked very expensive with a wealthy looking clientele sitting at tables overlooking the beach.

Feeling rather conspicuous among the casual smartly dressed customers, with our weathered clothes and wild hair, we looked for a table overlooking the beach, which wasn't already reserved. It was lunchtime and most tables had a reserved notice on them. There was one with a good view and we hastily sat down. We studied the menu and found the fish and chips were over twice the price we were used to paying. Watching the dish being served at tables nearby, we decided that we didn't want such huge portions or we wouldn't have been able to continue walking.

'Shall we share?' asked Karen.

The waitress came to the table and we ordered one portion of fish and chips and an extra plate. Cutting the fish in half there proved to be plenty. It was delicious and we shared sticky toffee pudding to finish the excellent meal. Notwithstanding half the regular price! We left a tip to show our appreciation, as the young waitress had been very polite and didn't turn a hair at our unusual request of sharing both dishes.

Repleat, with our satisfying meal to sustain us, we made our way up the rugged coast. The sun began to set as we approached Cape Cornwall. The area we found ourselves in had the appearance of having been quarry workings of some sort in the past. Among the ash paths tucked out of sight of the main route, we discovered a grass bottomed quarry. This was to be our sleeping place. Making sure our site was not too near the quarry walls to avoid the danger of falling rocks, we made up our beds. There were remnants of open fires surrounded by soot blackened stones, so we concluded that this place was a spot for locals, or other nocturnal visitors, to have barbecues and other secluded meetings. We just hoped they didn't plan to have such a gathering on the night we had chosen to sleep there!

The night had been warm and we had a good sleep. Needing a good breakfast, we headed for the village of Pendeen as we hoped the shops would be open by the time we got there, or there may be a cafe. Luckily, we found Heather's Cafe and sat down to a very good cooked breakfast. There was a farmers' market going on and we watched the animals being herded into pens and the auctioneer's jabbering, singsong recitals filled the air. Burly Cornish farmers pushed and pulled the animals, sheep and cattle baahed and mooed and the market filled the village with a life and energy which woke up it up from its usual sleepy atmosphere.

As we continued on our way, a group of young men came towards us walking in the opposite direction. They appeared to be Asians and seemed to be fascinated with us. They asked where we were making for and where we were staying. They were polite and friendly, so we explained about our travels. One of them asked if he could take a photo.

'Why do you want a photo?' asked Karen.

'I want to show my grandmother.' He smiled.

We laughed afterwards, as probably, his grandmother would have been surprised to see two ladies, maybe much older than her, clumping along the path carrying huge bags and sleeping under hedges. We met a few people who wanted to take our photos including an American man who was walking with his wife in the opposite direction to us. After a friendly interchange as we passed, he rushed back to ask if he could take our photos. We asked if he was planning to exhibit on social media and he insisted not. He probably wanted to show folk back in the U.S what eccentric old people lived in England and what they got up to. Anyway, there seemed no harm in him so we consented.

After a comfortable night sleeping in a field near Treen, we diverted to Zennor to find breakfast. There was only one place open so we had some expensive muesli before walking to St Ives where after eating a baked potato lunch we set off towards Hayle. On the way a man carrying a large rucksack hailed us. We got into conversation with him and discovered that he had recently retired and was fulfilling a long-held ambition to walk the Path. His wife was not a walker so he was journeying on his own. Unlike us he was using a tent and managed to find places to pitch it either on the beach, campsite or a space along the path. On the whole of our expeditions the few people we met walking the whole path, were mostly men on their own and in only one case a young woman in the army, who was using a bivvy bag like us.

The most unusual character we met was a fit looking man of about sixty, with a hippy appearance wearing sandals and shorts and a headband. He had all his equipment, including a tent in a not too big rucksack. He said he only used a small blanket to cover himself. I asked him how he washed, as his possessions seemed to be very limited.

'I go in the sea,' he said, 'I clean myself with coconut oil mixed with a little tree tea oil.'

He demonstrated by rubbing his hands over his head including his hair. Indeed, he looked fine with nice tanned skin and brown sturdy legs. He also told us as that he massaged his feet in his tent at night, he said a little prayer to them thanking them for carrying him on his way. He was an unconventional, independent individual who seemed to co-exist with the landscape in a most natural way.

That evening we made our way to the estuary at Hayle. We decided to sleep on Porth Kidney Sands where there was a wide expanse of sand with dunes behind. As the light faded, we set down our beds where the wide beach met the dunes. A few dog walkers passed by, well away down by the sea edge. Darkness fell and we put our books away. The murmur of the sea provided the background sound as we drifted off to sleep.

Next day dawned bright and sunny. After a walk around the estuary, to Hayle we had breakfast then decided to go into the sea to freshen up. We were to catch the express bus back to Oxford at Cambourne next day so needed to get there by local bus from Hayle. Arriving in Cambourne in the late afternoon, we needed to find a suitable place to sleep. The area was built up, Cambourne being rather a bigger place than we were used to. It was similar to Helston but without the convenient country park in which to find a place to sleep. We walked down a lane out of town in the hope of finding somewhere. The idea was to find a suitable spot, go back to the town and have a meal at Wetherspoons then return to our selected spot. Others must have had the same intentions maybe without returning to eat in town, as investigating a likely looking field at the end of the lane I saw a discarded dirty sleeping bag near the hedge surrounding the field. This put us off our search.

'It may belong to someone who may come back,' Karen stated warily.

We didn't wait to investigate further, scurrying back up the lane as fast as our worn out legs could take us.

The only bed and breakfast we could find, which had vacancies or was not too far to walk to, was Wetherspoons. We booked a family room which was the only one left and had our evening meal at the hotel. We had our only indoor sleep of this trip except for the backpackers on our arrival. We were quite peeved as we already had a bath in the sea. However, as the price of the accommodation was quite high, we thought we would use the facilities and had showers which though quite relaxing were not as satisfying as our natural sea bath.

Pit Ponies and Seals

In late June 2016, we set off again, this time starting at Hayle. As usual in was drizzling when we alighted from the coach. We seemed to be cursed with bad weather. We left the town and walked up onto the high slopes leading up from the sea. As evening was approaching and the threatening clouds made it feel later than it actually was, we looked around for somewhere suitable to camp. A golf course stretched on the landward side so this was not a good area. There were still a few golfers on the course, consequently we had to search out of their view and look further on. The area was made up of sand dunes which was in our favour as we could hide in the hollows.

Eventually, we found a place, down the hill towards the sea. It was in a sort of hollow and had some low trees and bushes to hide us and to use for making a shelter. The resulting tent was erected by slinging the tarpaulin over a large branch overhead and securing the sides to other branches with guy ropes. One door was a mackintosh tied to one exposed side and the other sides were protected by our umbrellas wedged in and pinned with tent pegs. Out came the groundsheets, mats and sleeping bags and we had our home.

'I could live here,' Karen observed. 'Sea view, detached residence. What more do you want?'

It was raining quite heavily now but we were proud of our apparently, successful construction. The night of rain which followed, gave justification to our pride, as we kept dry. However, we had some overnight guests in the form of slugs, who we met in the morning curled up on our mats beside us.

As we continued up the coast towards Portreath, the visibility was poor as sea mist obscured the scenery. Here the landscape was bleak, with remnants of previous industry such as shaft towers and obscure iron objects littering the ground. It was interesting and we spent time examining some of them, guessing their purpose, and also investigating fenced off shaft entrances, wondering how deep they were. We discussed the dangers of sleeping out in such an area, would we disappear through the unfenced entrance of a shaft and maybe, or maybe not, ever been seen again? Beggar the thought. Instead, we found a stable headland and slept there, sleeping well but covered in dew in the morning.

Walking up the coast we got a bit lost in a quarry. The path was made up of what appeared to be spoilage from the mines, probably a good use for it. Among the debris, I noticed a larger piece and picked it up. It was, what looked to be a fossilised upper jaw bone.

'What on earth have you got there?' Karen came over to look.

'The teeth are too big to be human, although, they are like human teeth,' I observed.

The jaw was blackened with the surrounding path material. We discussed the possibility of a dinosaur and, eventually, decided on a pit pony as the jaw looked too narrow to be a cow. It was too heavy to carry and I reluctantly placed it on a large rock at the side of the path hoping that an interested person might take it away and maybe find out about it. Karen took a photo of it with the intention of identifying it when we got home.

Later, feeling in need of a bath and the weather having improved with the sun shining, we took to the sea at a sandy beach. I tried to wash my hair in the sea with some liquid soap I had in my pack. I thought the soap was a special sort that lathered in sea water, this proved to be a fallacy and no lather formed. I may have brought ordinary shampoo by mistake and this didn't work. The soap I had meant to bring was guaranteed to form a lather in cold sea water and was multipurpose for body, hair, clothes and dishes. So much for dispensing liquids into small containers in order to reduce weight. It might have helped if I had labelled the container. Anyway, we felt refreshed by our emersions even if we smelt a little salty and the salt appeared to condition hair.

A couple of nights were spent on headlands providing warm, cosy relaxing sleeps. One of these nights, just as we were going to bed down, we heard music drifting from what we thought to be the direction of Perranporth. There must have been a festival or some such event going on and Karen rose to the occasion and danced to the music in her pyjamas and boots. The music lasted well into the night but we were oblivious to it, as we slept under the stars with our now familiar soother, the sound of the waves.

After spending the next night at Perranporth among the sand dunes, we walked on to Newquay. The day was warm and sunny. The Gannel estuary looked so inviting, but many holidaymakers frolicked in small boats and rubber dinghies in the hot sun so it was going to be difficult to sleep out in such a populated place. I used one of the public toilets on the way and felt a pinching feeling on the top of my leg near the back. With horror I felt a small lump attached to me and pulled it out. It was a tick. Squashing it I disposed of it down the toilet. We later had a swim at Newquay and before we went into the sea, I asked Karen to look at the area where the tick had attached itself to me. Finding her special tick removing tweezers, she operated and removed the horrible pest's legs. If left in the skin, they could have caused infection or even Lyme disease in some rare cases.

As we had walked up the estuary from Crantock where we had eaten lunch in a cafe, we looked out for likely sleeping places for the night. There were a few places but there was also a number of people around as it was still quite early. Now, after our swim and a bowl of thick soup in a cafe overlooking the beach, we returned to the river to search for a sleeping place. There was a suitable place with a flat piece of grass which was surrounded by trees. The only trouble was it was near the river and we didn't know how high the tide would rise in the night. The last thing we wanted was to feel it lapping around our feet in the dark. It was decided to go out of Newquay and find somewhere away from the town.

As we walked up a street near the bus station, where we were to catch the coach home in the morning, we saw a sign on a big house "Backpackers Hostel".

'Shall we see if they've got any vacancies?' Karen said. We were tired and felt we needed a shower and we could actually have a breakfast even if it was simple. We went in and with luck there was a twin-bedded room available. So, we booked it for the princely sum of eighteen pounds ninety-five pence each. Dave the warden showed us to the room indicating the showers and a storage place for surf boards. 'Have you got a storage place for Zimmer frames?' I joked. Although I could have been serious, the knackered state we were in. We returned to Oxford the next morning having informed Dave that we would be returning.

Headlights and Hurricanes

It was later in the year in early September, hoping for good weather, we travelled by train to Newquay and then by bus to Padstow. Our optimism was to be severely tested by experiencing the wildest storm we had so far encountered.

After sharing fish and chips at Rick Stein's restaurant, which were delicious, we walked around the picturesque estuary towards Rock. Near the sand dunes we found a tree with conveniently placed branches which enabled a rather good bivouac to be constructed.

'Here comes the rain,' Karen said as we dived under cover just in time.

In fact, it rained most of the night. We were accustomed to bad weather by now. It seemed to wait for us to come to Cornwall and try to discourage us from sleeping wild. Most conventional people would have agreed and advised us to find a more comfortable way of pursuing our ambitions. However, it was not as easy to find accommodation where and when it was required as previously explained. Anyway, we enjoyed the freedom and challenge, but must admit, sometimes a comfortable bed would have been appreciated, especially when sleeping out with only a piece of plastic between us and the pouring rain.

Polzeath beckoned as a breakfast stop. The weather was showery but we made reasonable progress along the cliffs passing through Port Quinn in the late afternoon.

'We'll find somewhere to camp before Port Isaac as it will be too near the village,' I observed. 'We don't want *Doc Martin* to bump into us on his rural rounds, do we?'

Port Isaac being the place with the fictional name of Portwenn where the highly popular series of *Doc Martin* was filmed. Along the path there was the familiar boundary field wall topped by the usual tough grass and heather fronds. I climbed the wall and looked over, the land behind was rough with nettles, thistles and rough bushes. It was lumpy and no good for our needs.

'We'll have to put it this side,' said Karen reluctantly.

We knew that it was best to be on the other side sheltered from the prevailing wind coming in from the sea but had no option as the "mattress" was too lumpy the other side. We were lucky there was a wall, as the wind was rising and lying down with the tarpaulin over us was a bit daunting as the umbrellas would have blown away or inside out.

As we tied the tarp to the grass at the top of the wall, the wind got stronger. It was getting dark and we didn't have much time to finish the task. Eventually we completed the securing and settled into our beds. I had decided to wear my Yogi suit instead of a sleeping bag to try it out. The Yogi suit was a thick fleece purple onesie. It was so comfortable and made it easier to get into the bivvy bag.

As we settled down to sleep, we heard the sound of a vehicle approaching. I peeped out into the night and saw glaring headlights lighting up the path.

'We're going to be turfed out,' Karen said anxiously. 'It's probably a warden.'

'We'll tell him we'll go in the morning. I'm not moving now,' I whispered defiantly.

I held my breath and the vehicle sped past. The engine sounds receding into the distance. We sighed with relief.

'He must have been looking for that cow,' said Karen.

As we had walked down the path earlier on, we had seen a stray cow on the verge which had appeared to have escaped from its enclosure with the herd. Perhaps, it had failed to return to its field and the farmer was looking for it. We were safe, as he either hadn't noticed us or wasn't concerned about our presence.

During the night the wind blew with increasing ferocity in from the sea, the tarpaulin flapped alarmingly and flurries of rain beat down. I put my torch on. Karen was fast asleep despite the turmoil outside. One of the ties holding the tarp to the top of the wall loosened and broke free. I had visions of the tarp taking off, swirling about in the wind and disappearing over the cliffs into the broiling sea below, leaving us exposed to the elements.

I shouted to Karen to warn her of our impending fate. She slept peacefully on, unaware of the possible catastrophic rude awakening she might have. Jumping out of the bivvy bag in my Yogi suit, at least I could move reasonably easily without getting tangled in bedding, I secured the guy ropes to the grass clumps and shrubs at the top of the wall and pushed the pegs further into the ground outside. Amazingly the tarp didn't take off and we were spared a bad wetting. Karen slept on, oblivious to the situation. We later discovered that the storm was the tail end of a hurricane which had affected America. It cannot be said that we were living a dull life at the moment!

Next morning, we set off towards Port Isaac. Here we had a well-deserved breakfast of poached eggs on toast in a cafe just down the road from where the fictional Doc Martin lived. The public conveniences across the road proved to be convenient in more ways than one as we cleaned ourselves up before heading for the bus stop at the top of the village. A man cleaning the street near the bus stop told us all about the filming of the popular series whilst we waited for the bus to come. We told him that we were looking forward to coming back to Port Isaac soon to continue with our walk and see what more adventures we had in store.

Celebrities and Characters

The next section of the path was to be tackled in October 2017. Due to the time of year, it was impossible to sleep out so we decided to use bed and breakfast accommodation and youth hostels. Having stayed in a bed and breakfast in Port Isaac overnight, we set off towards Tintagel where we had booked a twin-bedded room at the youth hostel. Walking along the rugged path not far out from Port Isaac a man came towards us. He stopped to chat with a friendly smile. A dog walker who we had previously met had informed us that Tintagel Castle was shut due to filming.

Discussing this with our new acquaintance, Karen asked, 'Do you think we'll see anyone famous?'

The man whose face seemed familiar to me, smiled knowingly and went on his way.

A woman came towards us and asked, 'You know who that was, don't you?'

'I know his face, but can't place it,' I said.

It turned out that we had been talking to the actor who played Al, one of the star players in Doc Martin. We thought it was quite funny that Karen had asked him about the likelihood of meeting any well-known figures.

The film they were making at the castle appeared to be a children's film. We met some of the film crew further down the track and jokingly asked if they had any parts for hump backed crones. If they gave us a cloak each, we could have wrapped them around us and with the back packs could have achieved the look!

The rain had been on and off during the day and we were glad to reach the isolated youth hostel. The room was spotless and Karen kindly offered to take the top bunk, much to my relief, as I had had enough climbing for the day. We had bought a cold pasta ready meal each in the village shop and had cups of the tea using the tea and milk which was provided at the hostel. A quite elderly man, wearing shabby clothes, told us that he had come from the north, with his wife, for a break. He spent the day bird watching not far from the hostel whilst his wife did a little local walking. Each to their own I thought. The man had another talent. As, as we lay on our bunks reading in the evening, the sound of a lively jig, played on a violin, was heard coming from the communal sitting room. Curiously, we went to see what was going on. The man was perched on the edge of a table giving an impromptu concert to a few hostellers sitting around the room. There was no television, as is the case with most hostels and the man was providing the evening entertainment.

The Diamonds at Lynton

During October of 2019 and January of 2020, the section of the path between Minehead, which is the traditional finish, and Ilfracombe was completed. We decided to do it this way because it was more convenient as we used public transport. This time we used bed and breakfast accommodation as it was the wrong times of the year to sleep out. We were lucky at finding the ideal guest house in Lynton. Our hosts were friendly and welcoming. The food was excellent as we could have an evening meal as well as breakfast. The most convenient thing for us though, was that they provided an informal transport service when needed between the start and finish of the walks. This service was invaluable, as for much of the route there was no public transport, especially at this time of the year.

The section was completed during October and January without major incident. It was difficult in parts but because we were only carrying day bags, these difficulties were comparatively easy compared with what we had completed before or were to tackle later. We did struggle from Minehead, up the huge hill to the top, as we were carrying all the things, we needed at the guest house. This section has been well documented so needs no description but to say that the views over to Wales from Exmoor and the dramatic scenery at Countisbury Hill are awe inspiring. We completed the section up to Ilfracombe by staying at the same place in Lynton to start with and moving on to Ilfracombe to stay for the last bit. We even managed to extend the walk to Woolacombe so it reduced the distance we had to walk next time.

The Coronavirus hit the United Kingdom in January 2020. In late February, before the lockdown restrictions applied, we managed to complete the section of the path from Woolacombe to Bideford. We stayed in a guest house in Barnstable after travelling there in Karen's car. Although we enjoyed the walking, the trip was "tame" compared with our usual unpredictable adventures. However, more challenges were to follow. We had not done with excitement, soakings and near starvation!

Soaked but Not Sorry

Due to the coronavirus, the country had been locked down since March 2020. Nobody had been allowed to travel outside their locality. However, since the end of June, people in England could travel further afield, and Karen and I, both feeling trapped, decided to return to the path. We decided to travel to Bideford in Karen's car to reduce our use of public transport during the coronavirus pandemic.

In early July 2020, we planned to attempt the final section between Bude and Bideford a distance of about forty-four miles. This was hopefully to be completed in two trips. Thankfully, pubs and cafes were to be reopened with restrictions such as social distancing, hand sanitising and other safety measures in place to help stop the spread of infection. This was beneficial to us as it had been a daunting thought to attempt walking with no prospects of buying a meal or food anywhere, without in the latter case, walking miles inland to the nearest village shop, maybe to find it closed. Some parts of the path are so desolate and there are few, if any facilities for obtaining food even with no lockdown. The packs on our backs were heavy enough without carrying a larder too.

After some discussion, it was decided we would start at Bude and work our way towards Hartland Quay. We had heard that this was the most difficult section of the entire path, so we thought we would try to tackle it first and see how far we got. We knew there was a pub and cafe at Morwenstow so hopefully we could get at least one meal there. We would take some food in our bags and water. I had decided to fill my bottle from streams and use water purifying tablets. Karen was a bit suspicious of these and ended up carrying about a litre and a half of water. She also carried small tins of fish in her pack resulting in a really heavy load. I had to minimise my load as I had a medical problem exacerbated by carrying too much weight. I managed to reduce my usual heavy weight by only taking minimal clothing, meal bars, protein drinks in powder form and breakfasts in plastic bags. These consisted of Weetabix, rolled oats, prunes, dates, sultanas and dried milk all to be mixed with water in the bag and eaten with a plastic spoon from the bag. These proved to be very successful.

We set off from Oxfordshire arriving in Bideford at about midday. Karen had arranged to park the car in an overnight car park for a week to be on the safe side. The instructions at the payment stand were confusing and Karen had to phone the information centre for advice. We didn't want to have come all this way to have to find somewhere else to park. The lady at the information centre reassured Karen that the ticket was overnight for the week and we heaved a sigh of relief.

Waiting at the bus stop for the bus to Hartland we were interrogated by an elderly man wearing a mask. We were wearing them too as it was a compulsory requirement for travelling on public transport.

'Where are you off?' he demanded in a curious voice. 'Camping out?' he continued with the interrogation. 'Where you from?'

I told him we were going to Hartland then on to Bude to walk the path. He looked a bit bemused.

'I've got six acres of woodland. You can camp there,' he said.

He told us the woodland was near Oakhampton so I told him it was a little off our route but thanked him for his kind offer. An onlooker would have probably thought what an odd conversation we were having. Three pensioners, two bent double with huge rucksacks, all wearing masks, being offered a place to wild camp in the woods. In retrospect, I think he may have feared for our safety or maybe our sanity and thought we would be safer in his woods than climbing up and down the path at our ages.

We eventually alighted from the bus at Bude. Walking up the sectioned off street with arrows pointing up the street on the right and pointing down on the left. We kept in our section and landed up at Sainsburys where we purchased our evening meals in the form of cold takeaways. Karen chose roasted vegetables with couscous and I had a sort of beetroot salad which was mostly beetroot. Carrying our purchases, we set off out of town and up the path to dine out and look for a place to sleep. A large patch of grass with a low wall on one side provided a perfect spot. A family were flying kites on the grass. It was a perfect evening.

Along the path, we passed Sandy Mouth where people were sitting at tables spaced out to maintain social distancing. I contemplated buying an ice cream but resisted as there were a few waiting to be served and I wanted to keep walking as far as we could before bed. About three miles up the path before Duckpool we found our sleeping place. It was well off the path with low bushes and rough grass. It took us a little time to find a reasonably flat area. Everywhere was on a bit of a slope, but eventually a spot was chosen. The few people we had seen walking were drifting off and peace descended. We could hear the faint sound of the waves and the temperature dropped. I put my pakamac on for extra warmth and Karen dressed in her layers as she felt the cold more than I did.

As we settled down, it was still light and the sound of young voices broke the silence. The voices receded into the night and the damp air was freshened by a soft breeze. Sleep came, but as we had retired very early at about eight, I was awake during the night and observed scattered stars and the silhouetted cliffs against a soft grey sky. It was not really dark because of the time of year and the air was damp and scented with grass and earth. My face felt cool exposed to the night air but the rest of me felt quite warm encased in my down sleeping bag protected by my bivvy bag.

Next day, we made good progress at first, but as the terrain became more severe, we slowed down considerably. Up and down was an understatement, it was more like climbing a steep mountain then trying to avoid slipping down the other side. The scenery was spectacular. Huge green topped cliffs falling sharply into the sea below. White foamed waves plunged strongly forwards and sucked relentlessly backwards, grey stony beaches bordered the sea and out in the bays jagged, black rocks dominated the scene. Many a ship had been wrecked or lured by greedy or starving locals in years gone by their cargoes pillaged. We had to be careful not to admire the views too much whilst walking in case we tripped. Every now and then we would stop and look back to marvel at the distance that we had come and relish the views.

I filled my empty water bottle in a cascading stream and added a half a purifying tablet. A whole tablet was meant for a litre of water, so if added it to a smaller amount the water would taste too much of chlorine, or whatever was in the tablet. Morwenstow was near.

'Shall we go to the pub and try and get something to eat?' I asked.

'Yes, there will be nowhere else,' Karen answered.

We were sitting on the grass resting after a heavy climb. A group of four people approached, probably two sets of partners.

'Come far?' asked a tall man carrying a long wooden staff.

We told them we had come from Bude and they were fascinated to hear that we were sleeping out without tents. They gave us directions how to get to the pub, bad directions as it turned out. They also told us where to find Hawker's Hut which I had read about and was keen to see.

The hut had been built into the cliff by the eccentric vicar of Morwenstow in the Victorian times. He used to sit in it and look out to sea. We found the path to the hut fronted by a large granite slab saying the hut belonged to the National Trust. It was a fascinating simple structure of weather bleached rough planks with strong latches to secure the doors. Inside there were weathered benches to sit down. There was just enough room to sit and look out to sea. Below, the cliff dropped in a steep fern filled gully to the sea a long way below. One could imagine the vicar, who apparently dressed in odd clothes, sitting gazing out to sea or perhaps writing a stirring sermon.

Now for the pub. The group had informed us that there was a tea room open too. We set off along the path looking out for a turn right to the village. There was a path which Karen thought might be the right one. It was well defined but crooked and went through a gap into a sheep field, we ended up at a dead end in another field with no continuing path and no sign of an exit. The sheep lined up and looked at us indignantly, not scattering and baaing as they usually did. We retraced our steps, eventually finding the path lower down.

We made for the church and found a sign informing us that the Vicarage Farm Tea Room was open. Seeing a few parked cars, we thought that the pub may be full, as when I had phoned before we left on the trip, the man answering said that it was advisable to book. Looking at the tea room menu pinned near the open hatch, we saw that soup was being served so we decided to eat at the tea room, not the pub which was about another ten minutes up the road. We had to sit on trestle tables outside and Karen brought the teas to us. The soup, tomato and roasted vegetable, was brought out by the waitress and it was delicious.

I had noticed on the map, a way to avoid the next deep valley, the head of which Morwenstow is situated. It appeared to go down through the woods by the church and emerge on the other side of the valley. This would avoid the steep descent and ascent and save our aching legs. Such is our luck, when we got to the sign pointing the way, there was a notice stuck over the symbol saying that the path was closed due to Covid-19. It appears that the right of way runs through a private garden and the owners had got permission to close it. So, we set off to find the way back to the original bit of the path we had diverted from. An arrow pointed trough the churchyard so on the way we looked in the church.

There was hand sanitiser provided so we used it. We probably needed it more than most people as we had yet to have a wash from sleeping out! We had of course sanitised our hands frequently with our own supply. The church was very impressive with fine architecture and ancient grey stone. Local people had made collages which were on display. They looked too sophisticated to have been done by children. They were of local buildings, historical characters and scenes and made a colourful feature to add to the beautiful stained-glass windows and ancient grey stone walls.

Continuing towards the path, we had to get over a farm gate as it was locked. We had obviously diverted again. Some people following us appeared to be lost too unless they thought we knew where we were going. We let them climb the gate first as they were not weighed down like us. I threw my bag over and gingerly climbed the wobbly gate. Karen squeezed through a hole made by someone breaking the middle bar of the gate. There was a young couple heading up the cow rutted path overgrown with brambles and ferns on the other side of the field's fence. A panicking sheep ran frantically to and fro in front of them bleating loudly. It had managed to get through the fence and couldn't get back to the field. The couple stopped to talk to us and the sheep calmed down and rushed up the path to find its' way back into the field.

'That's the wrong path,' I said. 'It's too overgrown.'

The man consulted his map.

'No, it's the right one on the map.'

It appeared that he was right but the path was abysmal, no wonder the villagers and others used a variety of haphazard paths to reach the village. The couple were from Lancashire and seemed to be doing a circular walk. They were making for the pub to get lunch. We met them again later on as we lay collapsed on the grass during one of our rest periods. They had managed to eat at the pub without booking and were on their return journey to their car. A walker appeared from nowhere and joined in the conversation. She seemed to know the couple as had probably met them earlier. She was walking alone on a circular walk too. Her husband was meeting her in the car. His knees were not up to the terrain she explained. She waved goodbye as she bounded off with surprising energy. The couple warned us that the next bit was a bit "hairy". Further on, we had to descended into the valley. The terrain was rough and we got a bit lost in a field as there were no arrows to point the way and no apparent style or gate by which to leave the field.

After wandering about, we found an opening in the hedge right in the corner obscured from view by scraggly bushes. There seemed to be a path of some sort which led to a steep incline. The surface was hard mud with little to hold on to. It would have been virtually impossible to go down in the rain if the path was slippery. I wondered if we had come the right way but could see two-foot bridges crossing a stream in the valley below. At one point, Karen sat to wriggle down as it was so steep.

'You will have to sit here,' she said. 'No, it's okay.'

She managed to stand and go forward. The path then seemed to go right to the edge of a crumbling cliff edge. There was a sheer drop, goodness knows how far down to the sea below. Luckily, as we neared the precipice, we found a new little path had been made further in.

'Thank goodness, I couldn't have gone around so near to the edge.' I felt relief wash over me. 'We must be mad. How many people of our age would be doing this, dicing with death?'

'Well, it beats sitting knitting or sleeping in the chair waiting for the next soap to come on TV. At least, for us it does, although most folk would disagree,' Karen said.

Proceeding along the path over the little footbridges, we came out into another field with easier terrain. The couple from Lancashire had told us about a writer's hut up on the next cliff. It had belonged to a renowned poet who lived in the valley and used it to write poetry and other works.

'You could sleep in it out of the rain,' said the young man. 'It says they lock it at night but we've heard they don't bother.'

I was intrigued and said we would visit it on our way. We reached the hut after a steep climb and went inside. There was a notice on the door saying that the hut was open to visitors and people who wanted to use it to write in but "no camping". Karen, being more law abiding than me, wouldn't consider us laying our beds on the floor, even though the forecast informed us that we were in for a night of wind and rain. Also, we might be locked inside if nobody checked inside if they did lock up.

'Well at least we can have our tea inside,' I said grumpily. Karen, who had a tin of sardines in her bag for us to share, wouldn't agree to this either.

'We'll stink the place out,' she said emphatically.

So, we ate our fish on the bench outside among the nettles and ferns.

We did view the hut before we left. It had such character. Old wooden benches and a table of the same weather bleached wood. Faded photographs were on the wall and samples of the poet's work. The views from the windows were spectacular cliffs, rocks and sea, wild and inspiring. The windows were set in the hut with no latches so could not be opened. No doubt if left open in a gale, it would cause havoc to the hut's contents.

Reluctantly leaving the hut as a young couple had arrived to view it, we carried on up the steep incline to the top. The wind hit us as the shelter of the valley was left behind. A man was coming through the gate in front of us. Two little dogs scurried through with him. He stopped to talk. He seemed very interested in what we were doing. He told us he had run the whole coast path in his youth, in fifteen days. It was amazing, here were we taking nearly ten years to complete the same distance!

'We are looking for a good place to camp,' I said.

He immediately offered us what turned out to be good advice. The next valley was the ideal place he said. He explained in detail where we would be sheltered from the wind. There was also a clear stream running through where I could fill my water bottle. Karen was yet to be convinced about drinking from streams despite using water purifying tablets. I think she was waiting to see if I survived the practise without succumbing to diarrhoea or griping stomach pains. So, we set forth to explore our new overnight accommodation, regardless of the weather front coming in.

Unfortunately, the place he had indicated had evidence of drug use. A few silver-coloured empty tubes lay about and other small bits of litter. The remains of a fire surrounded by large sooty pebbles spoke of a gathering of probably young drug users. We abandoned the idea of sleeping there, even though it was indeed sheltered, being behind a large grassy mound. We chose another place nearer the sea but more exposed. Karen lay on the floor to see if she was out of the wind.

'It's a bit better, but don't know how it will be if the wind increases.'

At that moment a car pulled into the little dirt car park where we had noticed the couple, we had seen at the writer's hut had put up a tent. It was the man who had directed us to the camping spot. He was checking on the couple and made his way to us. Explaining about the paraphernalia in our original site the man apologised and very kindly offered us shelter in his family cottage in the village about a mile inland. We declined his offer as we didn't want to impose on him or his family.

'Well can I bring you anything?' He was insistent.

So, I asked if he could bring a little milk in the morning. He left saying he would come in the morning and if we got too wet, we were to come to the village to his house.

The wind did increase and as Karen returned from her comfort walk up the valley. We decided to vacate our plot and return to the "druggies den". Wrapping our beds and everything else in the ground sheets, we staggered to the other site. I fell over on the rough, long grass and ended up in a pile with my bed on top of me. Karen had sensibly left her bag to collect on a return visit. I had tried to carry everything together. I wasn't hurt as the surface was soft. I could have laid there and gone to sleep, I felt so tired. I found a plastic glove in my bag and cleared up the debris around the site, disposing it into a carrier bag. It was much more sheltered here so we set up our beds again positioning the tarpaulin over both beds and securing It in place with tent pegs. It was certainly more sheltered here and as we lay in our sleeping bags reading, the distant roar of the sea was less deafening. During the night, I could feel the prickle of rain on my face and I opened my umbrella and held it strategically to protect it. The hood of the bivvy bag had been tightened with its' cord leaving a small hole to breathe through. This opening was too small as though it stopped the rain coming in, it was difficult to get enough air and condensation gathered. I widened it and was able to breathe more easily. I glanced across at Karen in the gloom. She was clutching her umbrella, too.

'Are you awake?' I asked quietly, not wanting to disturb her if she was asleep.

'Yes, I've been to sleep, but my arm is aching holding the umbrella. I'm really toasty.'

We usually tied the umbrellas to a tent peg to stop them flying away in the night, but on this occasion, we hadn't so had gone to sleep clutching them hence the aching arms. They had to be placed at a certain angle to stop the wind and rain as much as possible so a certain amount of holding was necessary unless it was a calm night. Although we were sleeping out in the wind and rain, we were warm.

We got up at about five thirty as our friend was coming with the milk soon, as we had told him we were leaving about six. My sleeping mat was soaked as the rain must have come in from the side of the tarp. I had been sleeping in a pool of water. Karen was not too bad. My sleeping bag was a bit damp but not too wet. The bivvy bags had served us well. However, we had gone to bed in our clothes and waterproofs. My ruck sack, used as a pillow with its' rain cover over it, was soaked. The rain had seeped underneath to wet the underside, leaving the top under the cover reasonably dry.

A car appeared in the car park and our friend appeared bearing a most welcome flask of tea, bottle of milk and a plastic box containing slices of lemon drizzle cake which he had made. It was most appropriate that the village he lived in was named Welcombe. We drank the tea with gratitude bagging up the cake to eat later. Waving goodbye, with promises to keep in touch, we set off up the steep hill out of the valley.

We sat further up the hill in a sheltered place and ate our breakfast. I used the remainder of the milk to put on one of my serial bags. It was delicious eaten in the wind and drizzle halfway up a hill. At the top, we experienced the full blast of the gale. It was ferocious and nearly blew us over. Drizzle showered us in gusty wettings and we plodded on through the sea mist which obliterated everything.

'Just our luck, we have the usual weather we seem to be fated with,' Karen shouted above the wind.

The man had informed us that it was reasonably flat for about four miles, with one more deep valley before Hartland Quay. As the weather was so bad with no promise of a let up yet and our bedding wet, we decided to make our way inland to Hartland and catch the bus back to Bideford. It was a hard decision to make, but with rain forecast that night again and sea mist obscuring the views, not to mention the strong winds, we decided to be sensible and return.

A few miles up the coast there was a path inland to Elmscott, from there it was about four miles by road and lanes to Hartland where we would wait for the bus back to Bideford. The path proceeded along the cliff edge and looked to be infrequently used as it was bounded by rough long grass and very narrow. It turned inland and passed a cordoned off area with tall wire fencing encasing huge satellite dishes. There was a field which we had to pass through in front of the fence. The field was full of cows and calves. We could see the gate out of the field in the fence at the other side. Among the cows was a huge bull.

'Don't like the look of him,' Karen said stopping in her tracks. 'They are supposed to be alright if they're with cows,' I said with false confidence. 'Let's go up by the fence and go past them. Don't look at them.'

This, we did, and the bull who was more interested in the cows, ignored us. We rushed through the gate, glad to get out of the field.

After some relatively easy, but wet walking we saw the turning to Elmscott. The lane turned north and we eventually emerged at the picturesque hamlet of Lymebridge which has lovely cottages and a sturdy stone bridge over a rushing stream.

'Shall we try the cake? I feel in the need of sustenance.' Karen sat on the bridge. The lemon drizzle cake was delicious and we finished it between us. We found that we needed to eat quite frequently as we found that "little and often" was better than larger meals spaced out. Not that we had much chance of larger meals on this stretch of the path.

We headed for what looked on the map like an unfenced hard surfaced lane. We ended up on a muddy farm track which led into a farmyard. A large man, presumably the farmer, appeared from a barn.

'You go up there.' He indicated a steel gate. 'Head for the church.'

There was no church in sight and we walked up a twisting cobbled path through a wooded hill. The path was like a medieval road and you could imagine peasant farm workers of long ago walking back from their day toiling on the land. Eventually, we saw a church and emerged into another pretty small village named Stoke. This village was only about half a mile from our original target of Hartland Quay. From here it was approximately a mile and a half miles to Hartland.

At Hartland, we found a pub open and ordered pots of tea before catching the bus to Bideford. Here we changed our damp clothes in the car park toilets before our return to Oxfordshire. We had managed to walk quite a distance in a day and two half days, considering the bad weather and difficult terrain. Not bad for two elderly ladies carrying heavy bags in adverse conditions, Karen's load being exceptionally heavy. We had to indulge ourselves with praise, as most people thought we were completely mad!

The Journey Completed

Karen drove her car to Bideford for our last section of the path in early September 2020.We parked up in the overnight car park as we had in July. Changing into our walking boots we set off towards Appledore. What a delightful village. We saw some huge earth works into the side of the cliff where a man was working.

'What's happening here?' I asked curiously expecting the site to be a block of holiday flats or large hotel.

He was building a house which was to have splendid views over the River Torridge. A wonderful location. The narrow streets of Appledore were difficult to negotiate with quite an abundance of vehicles coming up. On the front, overlooking the river, there was a cafe open. This was to be a rare occurrence, we were to find, on this last leg of the journey. We had to don our masks, order tea in one section of the cafe, follow the arrows on the floor to the exit and collect our tea from another part of the cafe. The coronavirus has certainly altered the habits of the nation. We sat outside opposite the cafe to drink our tea on socially distanced tables. On the outskirts of Appledore, we missed the path leading onto Northern Burrows Country Park and were on our way to Westward Hoe when we met a young woman with a dog. I asked the way onto the park and we had to retrace our steps until we found the entrance.

We had considered sleeping out in the park but it was too early and quite exposed also there may have been a ranger to turf us off. We sat on a seat for a rest and a man approached with two cuddly looking dogs. One proceeds to lift its leg over my rucksack. Just in time I shooed it off. The owner called half-heartedly for it to come back. He was a bit huffy that I had shooed it. Presumably, it was alright for his dog to urinate where it wanted to, but I didn't want to walk on with a smelly bag. I needed to fill my water bottle and we met a young ranger outside the toilets. Enquiring if it was okay to drink the water, she said better to fill it from the tap outside provided for dogs, as this was from the mains. As an afterthought she mentioned to be a bit careful as sometimes the sheep licked the tap. I wiped the tap and filled my bottle as there were no shops or any other way of getting water in the area. It was worth the detour however, as it is a beautiful area with views of the river and sea and towns and villages could be seen for many miles up the coast.

As we left the country park, the light was beginning to fade. It was always a bit difficult at this time of the year, as we had to find a place to sleep before darkness descended and this was about eight o'clock. It meant that we had long nights as it didn't get light until about six. I had brought a book to read by head torch light but only used it once on this trip as we were absolutely knackered by eight o'clock. Today, we had walked for about six hours but on full days we would walk from about eight in the morning, after eating our breakfast and washing with wet wipes and packing our gear, until about seven thirty when we found our sleeping location.

Now for a place to sleep. The path continued after leaving the end of the promenade where we had emerged from the country park. A mile or so along we discovered a flat piece of land overlooking the sea. It had evidence, in the form of charred logs surrounded by a circle of pebbles, of previous use as a camping or barbecue spot. There was a large mound on the sea side to provide shelter from the wind blowing in from the sea. We had found that it was not always the case that a mound or rocky outcrop provided shelter, as the wind had a habit of coming in either direction around the obstacle and we were as exposed as if there was no protection at all. This happened on our first night when the wind increased to gale force and whipped the tarpaulin covering us to a noisy, flapping tormentor.

'I can't hold it.' Karen was holding on for dear life. Luckily, we had secured the bottom with a large piece of wood lying across it.

'We will have to lie on it,' I shouted above the roar of the sea below. The wind was strong, there was no option. So, I dozed with my bivvy bag hood billowing around my head if I turned to face the wind. Karen seemed to sleep a little more soundly in the gale.

We emerged from the bivvy bags around six and as the wind force seemed to have dropped a little, managed to eat breakfast. Our breakfasts were a concoction of Weetabix, porridge oats or bran flakes, dried fruit, prunes, maybe chopped banana if we had any and dried milk all in a plastic bag. Water was added and the bag shaken vigorously after tying the top. The result was a good filling breakfast far superior to our previous packets of porridge oats with cold water. We ate it from the bag with a plastic spoon. I had a good seat on a large driftwood plank despite it wobbling a bit on metal fittings pierced through it. Maybe it had formed part of a wrecked ship from years ago.

The next part of the path was difficult terrain. At Peppercombe we met a man and woman, both retired army veterans but only middle aged. They were not together as the man was going in our direction and the woman the opposite way. They had both walked in many countries and the woman was going to walk to John O'Groats when she had finished the path. She told us that she had been walking with Paddy Dillon, the author of *The South West Coast Path* guide book further back along the path. I hoped we would meet him as I use his book a lot to find out difficulties that we may encounter along the route.

At Buck's Mill, we found a hatch open in a cafe and bought tea and ice cream. The man in the cafe said that I could fill my water bottle from a tap behind a sliding door opposite the cafe. There was a young woman and her friend buying refreshments. One of the girls had walked from Gloucester, camping on the way. She was making for Penzance. Wishing her a good journey, we continued on the difficult path eating blackberries on the way. A man was walking towards us down a slope. He smiled and said hello.

'Are you Paddy?' Karen asked as he was wearing the characteristic hat we had mentioned talking to the army woman. He acknowledged that he was and we had a talk with him about the route and our various experiences.

Approaching Clovelly, we were tiring and knew we would have to find a sleeping place soon. The surrounding landscape was not promising. The path we were on was named The Hobby. It was damp and gloomy with huge forested banks on either side and squawking pheasants scurrying madly around the stony path. The path, or lane as it was, seemed to go on forever. A couple we had met further back, said that it had taken them an hour to go from one end to the other. My feet were aching and muscles were sore. Karen's bag was digging into her lower back. We were a sorry pair. Eventually we emerged from The Hobby and sat on large stones at the start of a cobbled hill leading down into the village. We ate some broken biscuits and Karen the last of her sandwiches to give us a bit of energy before continuing. I had never been to Clovelly and was keen to see the village. I walked a little way down the hill, but not much could be seen, so decided to abandon the idea. We had walked up and down enough hills today and our legs could not cope with much more.

The map showed that the path seemed to run along the edge of the parkland of a large manor house, marked on the map as Clovelly Court so we set off to find the entrance.

'It should be on the left down the hill,' I said hopefully. We trudged down the steep hill until we saw a large ornamental gate on left. It seemed to be a drive leading to a house. There was no sign for the coast path. Further down the hill, there was still no sign for the path until at last we ended up at the bottom of the hill in a harbour area with a pub alongside. Asking in the pub where the coast path entrance was, the young woman behind the desk said it was near the top of the hill through the ornamental gates we have passed. Telling her that there was no indication that the path went through the gates, we asked if there was any food such as pasties for sale as we fancied something savoury and meals were pre-booked. They had a search and said there was nothing only chocolate bars or suchlike. Disappointed and fuming that the path hadn't been marked, we trudged back up the hill and entered the gate.

It was getting dark and we had to find a sleeping place soon. We found a place where the path through woodland had a large parkland area above it. There was a convenient hedge for cover so we arranged our ground sheets and bedding behind it so we were not visible from the parkland. We had to use torches as darkness had fallen. After what seemed an age of fumbling in the dark with only the light of head torches, we managed to wriggle into our bags under the tarp. Midges were biting so wearing the mosquito nets made the night appear darker. What a performance, it was almost as energy draining as climbing up one of the hills!

It was a good spot, with a hedge for shelter both from the breeze and as cover from early morning runners in the parkland above. A few spots of rain fell in the night and I fumbled about with my hand feeling for my closed umbrella alongside my bed, only to find that the rain stopped as I unfurled it. Karen had kept hers open just in case. The umbrellas proved to be useful on still nights as it felt like being in a tent, but were no good when there was a strong wind. We would tie them on to a tent peg in case they blew away, but they had to be at a certain angle so the wind didn't get under them and they protected us as much as possible. Consequently, one had to hold the handle whilst sleeping making it difficult to turn over in order to relieve aching elderly joints. Turning over itself, that night in particular, was a feat in itself. In order to keep as warm and dry as possible, we had resorted to sleeping in clothes, macks and leggings and as mentioned before, Karen wore her boots. This night I was so overdressed, I could hardly turn over. I was also too hot. In the morning I found that I was lying on the grass, off the sleeping mat, my head about two feet lower than I had started. Karen said she wondered where I was for a minute.

As we left Clovelly, we saw a stone shelter on the edge of the cliff. A man was sitting there among his bedding and rucksack. He had spent the night in the shelter as he was using a bivvy bag like us and the shelter had provided a suitable place to sleep. He told us that he had done charity walks and had taken to walking this time due to the uncertain economic situation the country was going through. Walking on, it began to rain with a vengeance so we were soaked for a while. However, the weather improved as we made our way towards Hartland Point. A young woman was walking towards us. We had met her further back and she was returning from the point. She told us she was camping a mile beyond Clovelly so by the time she walked back she would have done about eighteen miles. But we consoled ourselves, she was young, very fit with only a small day bag whereas we were old enough to be her granny, carrying huge heavy bags and still managed to achieve distances of ten to twelve miles in a day, even if we could hardly walk at the end!

Harland Point proved to be a success from the point that we managed to buy large cups of tea and crisps from a kiosk. I promptly spilled the tea over my trousers but the lady in the Kiosk replaced it free of charge. She told us that business was uncertain due to the virus hence the lack of choice of things to eat. The crisps were much appreciated as I think I needed the salt.

It was decided that we would walk towards Hartland Quay for a mile or so and find somewhere to sleep. The terrain was easier here and I suggested the edge of a field off the path a little with a hedge on the seaward side. Karen suggested we go on a bit as there was a flattish green area with stubby bushes ahead. It had a large sweep of land on the seaward side which may offer protection from the wind, but was visible from all of the surrounding area. Then we saw some pretty sheep trotting ahead of us towards the plain. They were joined by more on the way.

'Ticks,' Karen said, 'we had better go back to the field.' We parked ourselves on the edge of the field and we were pleased that we could see Lundy Island from our beds. The sun set with a myriad of colours, shades of orange, pinks and dark and light greys. The fading light eventually obliterated the colours and a few stars began to shine in the dark sky with a few darker rain clouds scudding across.

The last lap of the journey started with an easy walk along the plain we had viewed the night before, followed by a precarious scramble up a small mountain. Karen made the accent with comparative ease, I with more difficulty. We sat on a seat at the top and looked at the magnificent views. From here to the quay was quite a challenge. We passed the ruin of a tower and took photos of Stoke Church through the arch. We reached Hartland Quay with a feeling of achievement and triumph. Unrolling the banner that Karen had made from a scarf with a poster attached to it printed with the words:

2012 FINISHED 2020

630 Miles

South West Coast Path

We waited until we could find someone to take our photos holding the banner. A woman in a wet suit came up from the quay where she had been swimming with a group of wild swimmers. Explaining what we wanted, she said that she would be delighted to oblige. I told her to get changed first, so she left us saying she would be back soon. Meanwhile, a couple passed by and asked if he could take the photo. He did and the first lady came back and did the same. The pub had just opened so we went in and celebrated with a cup of tea. It was too early for meals and we had to make our way back to Hartland to catch the Bideford bus using our "pensioners" bus passes, of course!